WORKPLACE
WARFARE

WORKPLACE WARFARE

Break through Bureaucracy and Love Your Job Again

ANN D. CLARK, PHD

iUniverse LLC
Bloomington

Workplace Warfare
Break through Bureaucracy and Love Your Job Again

iUniverse books may be ordered through booksellers or by contacting:

iUniverse LLC
1663 Liberty Drive
Bloomington, IN 47403
www.iuniverse.com
1-800-Authors (1-800-288-4677)

ISBN: 978-1-4759-9484-1 (sc)
ISBN: 978-1-4759-9486-5 (hc)
ISBN: 978-1-4759-9485-8 (e)

Library of Congress Control Number: 2013913560

Printed in the United States of America

iUniverse rev. date: 10/10/2013

DEDICATION

This book is dedicated to the employees, past, present and future, of ACI Specialty Benefits in honor of ACI's 30th year of excellence. Rapper and record producer Jay-Z describes excellence as "being able to perform at a high level for a long period of time." This is ACI. Since its creation in a single home office to its now international presence, ACI has achieved numerous awards and recognition as a Top-Ten EAP, San Diego's Healthiest Company, and more, but more importantly has changed the lives of millions across the globe.

About ACI

ACI Specialty Benefits, celebrating 30 years of innovation, ranks in the nation's Top-Ten providers of employee assistance programs, corporate wellness, student assistance, concierge, and work/life services to corporations worldwide. With a 95% client retention rate and over seven million covered lives, ACI has provided personalized, high-touch service for 30 years. ACI remains a privately-owned specialty benefits corporation, headquartered in San Diego. For more information, visit www.acispecialtybenefits.com.

CONTENTS

ACKNOWLEDGMENTS

Although this book contains over 50,000 words, there are never enough to thank the many who have generously given time, support, and encouragement. First, to Adora Horton, whose creativity and criticism helped hone the final form, heartfelt appreciation. Aaron Grisafi, *Graphic Artist Extraordinaire*, skillfully and beautifully created the outstanding cover. Thanks to Rebecca Ann Jordan for her tireless editorial input. To Harry Chang, whose diligence in reading, developing, and editing made this book real, sincere thanks. Special appreciation to my daughters, Deanna Lynne Smith and Tandice DeShon Tinney, for their valuable technical advice and support with the original manuscript development. To the many interviewees, bosses, and employees alike, thank you for the generous gift of personal stories, time, and insights. To the corporations that have contributed to the ideas in the book, to the great employees who work there, and to the families who support them, thank you all.

INTRODUCTION

Reality shows have latched on to the drama of the workplace. Entrepreneur Donald Trump is firing apprentices in front of millions. Do you crave to see your boss squirm in *Undercover Boss*? Wish you could have more control in the workplace like *Does Someone Have to Go*? This book is for you. Viewers love these TV shows for a reason; everyone wants to be the boss, and employees want bosses to know what it's like to be on the receiving end.

When I was working as a high school English teacher, the principal of the school—let's call him Mr. Winkle—was a real micromanager. While I always had the requisite books lined up for the students to read, I also had slipped a few of my favorites (admittedly *1984* had once landed on the "banned books" list). Mr. Winkle exploded when parents called up in complaint. He insisted on a decades-old, outdated syllabus. If I deviated, I got an immediate slap on the wrist.

But I was stubborn. I kept my reading list. Some might call me a saboteur, but I thought of myself as a hero. After all, I was the expert—didn't I know best how to fill impressionable minds with great literature? It became a war I was destined to lose.

Warfare is not exclusive to military operations. It can take the form of a tyrannical boss, an alcoholic supervisor, job insecurity, competition between employees, clash of personalities, even unreasonable demands for time and effort. Add that to the stress already created by juggling home and family, constantly racing against time, and the personal sacrifices for work. The workplace can become a battlefield.

Workplace Warfare is about how to survive in the workplace without being eaten alive. It is a simple, practical, and workable approach to breaking out of the battles without wearing a Kevlar vest or taking a beating. Take control of your job and end the stress that affects not only daily productivity but your life and health.

Workplace Warfare contains real stories about real people with explosive problems who are trapped in what feels like a combat zone. It is about how to create choices when none seem to exist. It is about how to come to terms with the hostility that employees direct toward bosses or turn inward, causing ill health and unhappy lives. It is about amnesty, creating a demilitarized zone, and acceptance—with specific exercises and techniques designed to reduce animosity and anger, and the possibility of a violent and self-defeating response. It is about overcoming the crippling feelings of powerlessness.

The author of this book knows what it is like to want to grind a boss or coworker into the dust. I started my career with baby-sitting and my worst job was working in state government—the bureaucracy was deadly. Yes, I watched movies like *Horrible Bosses* and the classic *9 to 5* to get ideas on how to deal with coworkers, managers and a simple lack of shared values in the workplace. I've been there when that last straw was descending—the back breaker.

I will speak in understandable terms, giving real accounts of workers revealing frustrations. The stories will support readers by relating to personal dilemmas. Frustration and futility is not the end of the experience. *Workplace Warfare* will discuss methods for coping with difficult behavior (some your own), putting into action workplace survival techniques, and giving practical and efficient tactics of regaining personal power.

Conflict in the workplace costs everyone; whether measured in mental health or the costs of goods and services, workplace conflict is truly a no-win situation. The loss of personal control in the workplace may be exactly what provokes the worker to strike out through crime—from petty pilfering to sabotage of expensive computer systems—and even violence that could tragically lead to death. In bottom line terms, resentment in its various forms costs American employers over $800 million a week. The cost is borne by the worker, not just the stockholders.

But the workplace doesn't have to be about revenge. In *Workplace Warfare*, there are easy and practical suggestions to help anyone discover personal power. Learn ways to manage yourself and others to achieve personal goals. Feel healthier and happier by taking control and getting on with the job.

At the end of each chapter is an action section labeled "Take It Back." It means recognizing conflict and powerlessness at work, responding strategically, and reinforcing new behaviors to keep combatants at bay. Steps will include exercises, tests, and tips. Each chapter is a plan for change—not only to get on with the job, but also to *take it back* and win the battle.

Taking control may be a simple process: step-by-step assessment, planning, and choices are just a beginning. It is not easy. Yes, I learned to take it back at that teaching job. I stopped doing what I thought was best and learned to communicate with my boss and my colleagues. Rather than sabotaging, I lobbied to change a rigid system. It took longer than I had wanted, but I no longer felt as resentful. I began to feel satisfied with my job again. I had won the war.

Your success depends on you
You have to steer your own course
You have to do your own thinking
You must make your own decisions
You have to solve your own problems
Your character is your own handiwork
You have to write your own record
You have to build your own monument—or dig your own pit.
Which are you doing?

B. C. FORBES
Founder, *Forbes Magazine*

ONE

The Dysfunctional Workplace—It's a Family

> *"Your work is going to fill a large part of your life,*
> *and the only way to be truly satisfied is to do what you*
> *believe is great work. And the only way to do great work*
> *is to love what you do. If you haven't found it yet, keep*
> *looking. Don't settle. As with all matters of the heart,*
> *you'll know when you find it."*
> Steve Jobs

There is a daily need to cope with disruptive forces in the workplace. Mergers, layoffs, unscheduled overtime, inconveniences, and changes that must be dealt with on a minute-by-minute basis are only a few of the challenges faced in the workplace. It makes little difference whether you've worked on a job for a few hours or a number of years. A manager walks by and gives the order that upsets the status quo. The company closes its doors with no notice. Uncertainty creates a sense that there is no control. Surely you have none!

Do your hard work and dedication pay off? Are these concepts that have gone out of fashion like a '70s Nehru jacket? "Sure, I like my job," you respond without hesitation. Then you ask yourself, "Do I like my boss? My uncaring, unconcerned, unbearable, unthoughtful, unpleasant, un . . . , un . . . , un of a boss?" How can you quit? You're not working here for your health after all. Besides, you're doing a good job. You've never been late, and you're faster than the others who perform the same tasks, but never once received a compliment. Often you feel you're treated like part of the equipment. You have no control. Or do you?

1

Sometimes we protest. Employees take out the frustration and anger in subtle ways. Have you left a customer waiting, ignored a telephone ringing, called in "sick" on a big day, taken long lunches, or swiped pencils, not because you needed to but because somehow it soothed your anxiety? You fought back. You felt some sense of power in the workplace. If only for the moment, you felt in control. What about the other workers and your work environment? Do you feel as if there's a gloomy cloud hanging over the employees? You are not alone; the negative games played within the company and by the boss are played in companies everywhere. Real workers, just like you, talk about their powerlessness.

A TALE OF TWO COMPANIES

"I have the perfect job," says Theresa, a petite brunette in trendy clothes. "Well . . . had it. I was a receptionist for a large defense contractor." Married to a state trooper, Theresa had a job that complemented his schedule and gave her time to be with their son, a senior in high school. "I worked four and a half days per week and was paid a significantly higher wage than the average receptionist. I had good equipment, friendly coworkers, minimum supervision, and excellent benefits. It really was a perfect job. Not only did I think it was perfect, I thought it was permanent. I held the job for over five years. Because I didn't want to go back to school, I was willing to be a career receptionist. I didn't want to upgrade. I didn't want a promotion. In some ways I thought this assured me of keeping the job. No one could be jealous of me and no one could want my job. What a surprise when the company announced a major reorganization."

With no notice, Theresa was thrown into the battlefield. She would now work five days a week and have more work. No more half days off. Her hourly salary was to be cut, and with the increased workload she got more supervision. Her job skills were not even adequate for the new supervisor; she received frequent oral and written warnings. Her life became a nightmare. How did this happen? Overnight the mission changed. She went from being the perfect employee with the perfect job to the employee from hell with the job from hell. Theresa now faced a tight job market with limited skills and the possibility of a poor reference. Or, she could adjust and endure.

Vic tells a different story, but he and Theresa have much in common. "To me, being called a workaholic was a compliment," he said. "I worked sixty to eighty hours a week as a vice president for a large corporation providing software to the automotive industry. Vice president was a level of promotion that I never thought I would achieve because I had no college or formal training. I was a good salesman and I knew the product. As the marketplace began to change, there was more competition and foreign intrusion. Our company fell into what I can only describe as a stalemate that resulted in panic, and that panic resulted in severe demotions everywhere."

Vic continued, "Company cars were taken away. Expense accounts were monitored. Smartphone plans discontinued. I was demoted, not just to a level below vice president, but down to a middle manager. Overnight I lost my company car, my laptop, my travel privileges, my secretary—all the perks of my job. More importantly, I lost my self-esteem and confidence. All the years of dedication and faithful service, the sixty to eighty-hour work weeks, and the total disruption of my family life were rewarded by the most incredible punishment."

Like Theresa, Vic experienced shock in the form of an abrupt realization that any security he had in his job was an illusion. Both Vic and Theresa had attempted to secure their places in the corporation; both worked hard and competently. Theresa believed her modest expectations assured her continued employment. Vic believed his "more is better" philosophy of being a workaholic gave him job security. Both felt untouchable and secure—in control.

These two stories dramatically exemplify how the workplace can become a battlefield for the employee. Too often the result is that the employee becomes the enemy or assailant in the workplace. These two employees felt that they had significant control over their jobs. They both felt that hard work, job competency, and loyalty would result in certain guarantees. They felt, as many of us do, like they had an unspoken deal with their corporations. They quickly learned that the other party had not signed on the dotted line of that deal. The workplaces that Vic and Theresa have just described were havens for them, providing not only the money that supported their lifestyle and enhanced their families, but also the right of freedom. Yet, overnight, the jobs became nightmarish—the employees felt trapped and powerless. Overnight, they were at war with the jobs they had previously loved.

All too often an employee sees the workplace as a battleground and himself or herself as a combatant on the frontline, under the command of several disruptive forces: economics, business trends, competition, foreign intrusion, or simply poor decision-making and mismanagement. It is the uncertainty and powerlessness of this, of all war, that drives workers out of control.

The Crime Prevention Manual for Business Owners and Managers warns that any given business may be losing as much as a third of its profits to internal crime and employee sabotage. Additionally, as many as 30 percent of all business failures are a direct result of internal theft, often due to employee discontent. So, why doesn't management listen? Why are stories like those of Vic and Theresa so common? To see where companies' self-interest diverges from that of its employees and, more importantly, what results from those discrepancies, let's look further.

THE SUGGESTION BOX

When Janice received the corporate edict stating that thousands of dollars had to be cut from the upcoming budget, she took her responsibility very seriously and came up with ideas for saving money. She met with her team and several good suggestions came forward. One of these suggestions included placing restricted phone lines in conference rooms where Janice had observed workers frequently making personal phone calls. With about twenty conference rooms, or twenty "free phones," in her building, she felt this could make a significant difference. Janice even went to the trouble of tallying the workers who entered a conference room area near her in order to document the possibility of savings.

Janice provided her data and suggested a review of the phone records for these conference rooms. Based on simply attributing a local toll call to the total number of unauthorized entrances to the conference rooms she came up with significant savings for just one conference room. Janice was very proud of her analysis and initiative. She and others submitted their reports for budgetary control to their own bosses. Several months later there was still very little feedback. But the increasing stinginess of the company became apparent. Janice was not allowed to replenish supplies, people were told to use pencils when they ran out of pens. There was a level of pettiness that seemed to agitate the workers and interfere with job performance.

Janice then went to her supervisor to ask about the status of her suggestion for controlling telephone use in the conference rooms. He informed her he had passed it on. She asked him to follow up. He said he would. Again, weeks went by. Morale was increasingly low. Janice decided to approach the chief financial officer (CFO) of the company in a casual and joking way to ask about her suggestion. The CFO was a very approachable man—unusual, Janice felt, for a "business type." Luckily, she had encountered him in the hallway, where she could casually ask if he had taken a look at her proposal.

The CFO laughed. "What if some bigwig wants to make a call, Janice?" he said. "What are we supposed to do? Tell him that we are saving money and they can't use our long distance lines?" Janet smiled and felt her cheeks turn red. She believed that her suggestion may have been laughed at behind closed doors. Janice made some light response and retreated.

She went back to her office cubicle and felt like crying. She wondered how she could have been so misunderstood. As she sat feeling humiliated and somewhat ashamed, she began to experience another feeling: anger. She pictured upper level management, cigar-smoking, scotch-drinking, immaculately groomed executives standing in the conference rooms, contemptuous of employees, contemptuous of money, contemptuous of the small savings that Janice and her coworkers had envisioned as being helpful to the overall mission of the company.

Her anger and rage grew. She sat in her office for a long time. She plotted various forms of revenge. She saw herself going into the conference room and placing long distance calls to friends across the country. She saw herself dialing random numbers so the calls couldn't be traced back to her. She sat for yet a longer time plotting. In an exchange that had taken only minutes, Janice had changed from a dedicated, goal-directed employee to an angry, resentful, and hostile team dropout.

Have you ever felt like Janice? As a worker, how often do you think that instability of the workplace makes it feel more like a battleground than a place to perform your duties? You try to rationalize their ideas. You try to talk it out with your supervisor. "Gee, boss, we sure would like some time on this one. Could we talk about how this will affect our work on the project? Do you have a few minutes?" you ask in your most confident, responsible voice. For moments that stretch to what feels like hours, you begin to feel droplets of sweat form on your brow, and you wait for the affirmative answer: "Sure, come in to the office right now. I've been wondering what you think." Then your eyes meet. There's the "who-the-hell-do-you-think-you-are" look in the boss's eyes. You instinctively know that means the decision has come down from the top. "I can't do anything about it," says the boss as she fiddles and restacks the papers on the desk. There's no possibility for an alteration in the program. The order is given. You walk back to your work area, frustrated and disenchanted.

A part of the scenario you might have missed is seeing the helpless emotion that crossed the boss's face when you left the room. She sat there muttering, "Gee, I know how it feels, but I've got my orders too. I'm stuck in the middle, just like the employee. But, I'm higher up without other coworkers to share resentments or responsibilities. Nobody ever sympathizes with the boss."

Hey, it happens to everybody. Welcome to life. Some workers handle these conflicts with aplomb. But truthfully, a large portion of the workforce, all the way up and down the corporate hierarchy, share overbearing feelings of anger, frustration, and powerlessness during trying times. You're not alone if you've lashed out at an employer's disregard for you. And you're certainly not alone if you've ignored those feelings of resentment, only to increase personal stress and discomfort. Exactly how often do you feel the pressure and workload of the job seize control of your mind? Do you force yourself to go against your value system? How frequently have you experienced the terror of thinking you'll be let go, publicly ridiculed, or intimidated by your boss? When you're sick and tired of feeling like an enemy combatant lost in the blast of improvised explosive devices, you must start a new battle—a personal battle to take back control. Acknowledging that you are your own best ally is the first step to fighting back to your rightful position.

A No-Win Situation

Connie is a single mother with two kids at home. She'll be ready to retire in five years. About three months ago, she heard through the grapevine that the plant would be opening a new facility inland, about one hundred miles away. "I worked twenty years for this really big snack food manufacturer. I toiled my way from the absolute lowest rung on the ladder into management. I'm proud of my accomplishment. It's taken dedication and pride in my work."

As she spoke, Connie bit her lip and focused on the scene in her driveway, her daughters soaping up the family's elderly station wagon. "When I heard the rumor from a reputable source, I talked it all over with the kids, and we agreed that changing high schools wouldn't be great, especially for Heather, who is a senior. But we're a family. We'd handle it. But when my boss finally called me into her office, I was told I wasn't going to be one of the people to move. They were demolishing my job. After twenty devoted years, I was phased out."

Connie stopped and twisted a button on her sweater. "They wouldn't need me in the new facility even though I wanted to go. I was willing to sell our family home, transplant my kids, change churches, and be unable to see my elderly parents as often. I was willing to sacrifice all that, and they still didn't care." Connie hesitated for a moment, squaring her shoulders. She was obviously a woman who had mastered plenty of hurdles. "The boss said she understood and gave me a choice, knowing that I'd lose my retirement and health benefits if I quit. They also offered me a year's severance pay, but no health benefits. They [the bosses higher up] started to hassle me. I'm too expensive to have on the payroll, I guess. But I continued to concentrate on my job.

"Then they made me this 'generous offer.' I could stay with the plant in San Francisco, but go back to the graveyard shift working in quality control—on a twelve-hour shift, no less. Since I was still management, it was somehow okay for me to work twelve hours straight. Sure I'm angry. But I'm going to stick it out. What real alternative do I have?" She went on, "I know it's not my boss's fault. She's just taking her orders from the management, who get their orders from the CEO, who then has to answer to the accountants or stockholders, who only see the bottom line. Sure, it's not fair, but that's business. Anyhow, who ever said that a company should be fair?"

Connie stopped talking. She rubbed her lips with the back of her fist, took a breath, and continued. "About a week after going back on the night shift, manufacturing potato chips, I started to reject every other batch of chips as they passed by me on the conveyor belt. I've been with the company so long; if I said they weren't right, not up to our quality standards, nobody even thought to question my decision. There was nothing wrong with them. The chips were fine. But seeing the chips being crunched up and on their way to the landfill made me feel good. Slowing the assembly line gave me a sense of power over the company.

"About a week later, while I was going over some procurement orders (I'm supposed to immediately review, initial, and transmit the orders to the warehouse for a regular shipment of chip bags) . . . well, I 'accidentally' spilled coffee on the forms. Now, they're at the bottom of my 'in' basket. They're drying. They might even get lost."

Connie now feels power and a sense of control. The action she has taken for revenge may pass. Or she may go further: close down the line, take her frustration out on the crew under her supervision, or worse. Connie is an employee out of control.

DON'T LEAD WITH YOUR FEELINGS

How would you have reacted in this situation? Would you have sabotaged one of the potato-chip ovens in order to slow production? Slashed the boss's tires? Quit on the spot, destroying records or equipment? Or would you have ignored the problem but soothed your churning insides with antacids, alcohol, or drugs? Would your family have suffered your irritability, temper, and general distress? Does job stress attack you in the form of ulcers, backaches, migraines, or depression?

Quite often, the effects of losing control and feeling like a pawn are registered in subtle ways. But subtleties in retaliation, such as Connie's "losing" of the procurement forms, can snowball into costly sabotage. The results of revenge rob the company of profits as well as take away an employee's personal self-respect. The extremes of Connie's reaction are a measure of the emotional distress she was feeling.

Remember, resentment, unchecked vengeance, and retaliation cost American companies in overhead that is passed on both to the employee and the consumer. Healthcare expenses can reduce net profits by as much as 50 percent, according to the Henry J. Kaiser Family Foundation. That price tag affects us all right in the wallet. As consumers, we pay higher prices for every product from insurance to detergent because of this sense of powerlessness and lack of choices to deal with workplace negativity that prolongs getting on with the job.

I'm not going to tell you to give up, be trampled, to keep smiling when your workplace is crumbling and turning into a hostile zone. I understand that feeling of impending danger, the hostility, the resentment and frustration of not knowing what will happen tomorrow. I'm not going to tell you to go back to school, color another parachute, and thumb your nose at the old boss when you are accepted as a mover and shaker for a large competitor. But this book will help you to focus on your own self-esteem, health, and emotional well-being in order to take control of what you legitimately can control.

It is the utter loss of personal control that invokes workers to strike out through crime, from petty theft to sabotage of extensive computer systems, or self-sabotage. It's the deprivation of being valued as a worker, feeling insignificant, that pushes some workers to lie, telephone their friends halfway across the continent, take home pens or Post-It notes, sneak out for two-hour lunches, or turn inward, stealing their own good health. Yet, Connie's boss has a boss also. He too may feel as you do. The ripple effect is taking its toll.

We label our feelings as frustration, anger, resentment, and fear. We try to get even or fight back against "the system." Health costs soar. Consumers eventually see it as increased prices. Revenge and anger in the workplace eventually affect everyone. But the only one you're concerned with is you. The feelings Janice, Connie, Theresa, and Vic have experienced happen to all workers at one time or another. You are not alone. Other employees are having the same emotions and similar responses. Perhaps, unbeknownst to you, they are the boss— enduring the same anger, the same frustration, the same feeling of being undervalued, the same malice toward his or her boss as the employees who experience it below them. Consider the personal price if you choose not to identify with your feelings. In the narratives, we saw how Theresa became hopeless. Vic lost not only his self-esteem but an entire lifestyle. Janice felt humiliated, and Connie compromised her personal values. All of them suffered severe stress reactions.

You have your own story and your own stress level. Like others in today's workforce, you might become a statistic as benefits in worker's compensation payments exceed the $150 billion per year figure. Or you can make some choices. Your situation may not be just like those described in this chapter, yet there are probably similarities. Look for those. Then make a consistent effort to use the techniques outlined. Actually write down your responses—don't just think them. As you progress you'll find you can successfully plan a strategy that works. You can gradually take control of your own behavior, take advantage of opportunities, and move toward accomplishing your goal, becoming more effective, more confident, and more of the satisfied and productive person that is truly you.

Take It Back

Recognize

Make one sentence to summarize what you want to change in your job situation. Theresa wanted her job to change back to the way it was. Vic wanted the market to change. Janice wanted recognition and validation of her creative efforts. Connie wanted a return to her old job. Each employee wanted to change something that was impossible to change. List what you recognize as the problems in your job. Don't limit the things that you can change. Brainstorm. Get it all out.

Respond

Respond now to the items you have listed. In this chapter, Theresa had control over her attitude. Initially, she saw herself as limited to two choices: quitting or taking the new schedule and responsibilities. By opening herself up to other possibilities, she could see more choices. She could increase her job skills through courses and schooling, seek positive evaluations from current clients, or build her resume—not just of jobs held, but of job skills. Then, she might feel more in control of the situation. Respond to those things you can change and list them here (attitude, job skills, career choices, etc.).

Reinforce

Now you develop steps to reinforce the behaviors you need to change in order to take control. What next steps are you willing to take? Here are some next steps in our stories. Theresa committed to taking a short course offered by her church on developing affirmations and positive attitudes. This reinforced her acceptance, as a first step. Vic not only began an exercise program but also joined a networking group of sales and marketing people with whom he felt he had good rapport and could be understood. This reinforced his commitment to take control of himself and make some changes. Janice decided to confront the CFO in order to let him know her feelings and seek a reconsideration of her very serious proposal. She also had begun a "no send" letter—one she never intended to mail. It outlined her feelings to the CFO. She was seeking to create a new context in which her humiliation had taken place. Good people can say stupid things; she decided to view him as an understanding person who simply misunderstood one situation. List the reinforcement actions steps you might want to take.

TWO

THE BATTLE WITHIN

"My first message is: Listen, listen, listen . . . to the
people who do the work"
H. Ross Perot

Frequently, when asked about the causes of on-the-job problems and dissatisfaction, employees say, "I love my job. I'm a good employee. Management is the problem." The answer begins with blame. According to the employees' point of view, management does not care about their personal goals, desires, needs, and wants. The feeling of being unappreciated increases frustration, and management becomes the target for anger. The boss may be the direct supervisor or merely an illusion: an unnamed corporate head that is perceived as controlling your very existence even down to getting a drink of water or using the bathroom.

Dustin, employed in a large hospital, relates her experience. "When the rumors about merger and layoffs began, we all began looking at each other as though we were enemies. I was reminded of something I read about Vietnam. Soldiers tried not to make friends with new replacements because they might be quickly killed. This may sound dramatic. I didn't want to see my friends get laid off, but the truth was, better them than me."

Another employee describes the effects of budget cuts. "It was like a medieval siege. We were so short on supplies; we all began hiding and stockpiling. I made a joke one day about an 'internal black market' so we could get our work done, and no one laughed."

CONTROL AND POWER

Control is an important concept in dealing with any situation in which a person feels real or perceived domination, threat, or intimidation by another. Yet, domination and intimidation are inherent in the workplace. According to the dictionary, control is "to have power over someone." Words like guide, restrain, and regulate are used as synonyms.

"Well," you say, "there's no news in that headline! The workplace certainly has lots of power over me. My boss, the owners, the stockholders, and the people under me consume my time. The people over me want all my energy. Everyone seems to have more control than I do."

Let's try to develop a more practical view of control as affecting those around us. Control is boosted by increasing influence and by increasing our feelings of power. And, much of what we perceive as controlling us—bosses, money, the economy—is not quite so black and white. While the boss controls us, the boss too feels controlled. The boss is susceptible to influence, to control. But do we really consider our own ability to influence these forces?

An important component of increasing control is to change our perception. Perception is reality. If we feel controlled, we are. If we perceive a situation in a certain way, that becomes reality for us. Our perception can be changed by events. Keep in mind philosopher Reinhold Niebuhr's wisdom in the Serenity Prayer:

Grant me the serenity to accept the things I cannot change, the courage to change the things I can, and the wisdom to know the difference.

BLAMING IS NOT CHANGING

For the first three months of her job in a chiropractic office, Georgia was on probation, as were all new employees. According to company policy, she was to be hired permanently or let go after a trial period of ninety days. Georgia, a gentle, demure young woman, was good with detail. However, she showed little initiative in going beyond the actual assignment, although the work she did with patient records was superb. Unknown to Georgia, the supervisor wanted more from her. The months passed. Georgia watched the calendar. She felt her entire life and financial security were hanging on the upcoming decision. Worry deteriorated her confidence level even more. She couldn't speak out, and she was terrified to ask about her employment status.

The administrator of the practice realized that regardless of her attention to detail, Georgia would have to leave. They simply needed a more "take-charge" individual. Within a week of the three "official" months of probation, Georgia was released. When she was told, her face paled slightly but she said nothing. They let her go without further explanation. They didn't even tell her that her last week's pay in the doctor's office would be held for twenty days until the paperwork was completed.

At the end of her final work day, Georgia had taken all of the computer hard drives with patient records. In her anger and frustration she tried to get even. Timid Georgia had showed them. But had she really? What did this malicious act cost her? She was bitter about how badly she had been treated but turned the anger on herself. Georgia had lost control, acting in a manner totally contrary to her values. The chiropractic practice sent her final check immediately, yet she still refused to return the hard drives. She could not understand her own vindictiveness and still did not speak out. The office didn't realize that keeping her on without telling her the status of her employment would drive her out of control. They dismissed Georgia as unstable, a kook.

The last time I talked with Georgia, she was still feeling angry, tense, depressed, and spiteful. The entire incident ate away at her. What she failed to realize was that she wasn't punishing the chiropractor or her administrative assistant (the office was again running at top speed). She had only inconvenienced her former coworkers, who were forced to clean up her mess and reenter all the patient records. Unlike the employees in the previous stories, Georgia could not see any alternatives to accepting her situation. Too timid to ask for feedback, she also did not confront her own shyness. She did not ask for help or seek to influence the course of her destiny. She viewed herself inwardly as a victim. And so she became one. Georgia was losing the battle within.

Baby Steps

Recently I listened to an employee describing a stressful challenge she was anticipating. Serrila had just joined a corporation as a sales rep with a six-month probationary period for new employees. The company had designed a week of what she described as tests, and at the end of that week the new representatives would be "up or out." There was tremendous pressure on her to perform. Not only was the workday to be filled with a series of tests, but in the evenings each employee would be on display during the socializing. Serrila had begun to feel anxious and tearful, and experienced nightmares in which coworkers were tortured by uniformed managers.

Even though this employee reported a good record of performance, her fears had totally altered her perception. She felt completely powerless. She saw herself as a child, being evaluated by teachers and parents with a report card that was dooming her to extraordinary punishment.

It seemed the employee was saying, "I need specific suggestions. I need to get my fear under control. I can't deal with this pressure and stress."

The first suggestion I made shocked Serrila. "You need to plan your wardrobe," was the casual response. She looked at me as though I belonged on the couch and she should be sitting in the comfortable chair giving advice.

"Plan my wardrobe? That's the last thing I need to worry about!"

"No, it is the first thing. You have total control and power over what you wear. Let's begin in an area in which you have control, in which you have expertise, in which you have confidence."

We proceeded to talk about taking charge of those things over which she truly had control, increasing her sense of personal power in order to offset the fear. In reality she did not know what this coming week would be like, and she had a history of success so far. She might not be the best sales rep, but she certainly was not the worst, according to her own admissions and objective evaluations.

Weeks later Serrila called back. She laughingly said, "My red suit was a big hit. You were absolutely right. Not only did I plan my wardrobe, I started exercising. I had put off all my exercise in order to learn the new inventory software. I took time out to go to the gym. You were right. I went into 'hell week' feeling confident, powerful, and very organized. I realized too that organization is very important to me. I had felt very disorganized because of all the pressure and the unknown demands. I'd had to prepare for everything, and as a result I was preparing for nothing."

She went on, "It was a very rough week but I got through it and I am going to be made a permanent employee. I'm really grateful to you for focusing me in the right direction."

This example shows a small but powerful step in which an employee was able to refocus fear, resentment, and anger at the higher-ups into action steps resulting in a sense of power and control. The employee had experienced self-empowerment.

FALSE EVIDENCE APPEARING REAL (F.E.A.R.)

Fear creates inaccurate mental pictures of future events, especially around our jobs. We also create expectations: Being an airline pilot is exciting, doing scientific research is dull, and working in a television studio is glamorous. Very often we don't ask enough questions to find out if the facts will confirm expectations or allay fears. Starting with false assumptions results in frustration, disillusionment, and resentment. Serrila's description of being overwhelmed by fear, stress, and pressure is an example of *False Evidence Appearing Real.*

Another example of F.E.A.R. begins with Carlos, unemployed for several months. He noticed a posting online: "Television studio needs production assistant. Will train." He thought of the glamour surrounding the media and all the celebrities he would meet. He called and arranged an interview for the next day.

Carlos was so overjoyed when he landed the position that he didn't read the fine print on the job description or listen carefully to the interviewer. At 9:00 the next morning, Carlos reported for his first day in the television industry. "So you're the new assistant, welcome aboard. How about running to Starbucks and grabbing me a grande latte?" the producer said. Carlos returned quickly, anxious to get started. "There's a bunch of old posters and pieces of scrap wood in the back room, Carlos. Take them out to the dumpster in the back of the building, and then sweep up. Find a broom." Carlos spent the entire day cleaning up and running errands. By Friday he was disenchanted and looking forward to a weekend off.

While checking out for the day, the producer approached him. "Carlos, we're a little short of staff this weekend. I'd like you to be here tomorrow morning at 8:00." *There go my plans for Saturday*, Carlos thought. *Oh well, I can use the overtime money.*

One week later, Carlos received his first paycheck. *This can't be right. I know I should have a bigger check than this.* He went to the boss, who explained, "You're on a monthly salary, not an hourly wage. There's no such thing as overtime pay for exempts." Carlos was angry, and he began to blame himself. He could have been spared the disappointment by finding out just what he was expected to do, how many days a week he was required to work, and how he was to be paid. Instead, he had created a false sense of victory, which caused him to lose an actual workplace battle.

THE ROAD LESS TRAVELED

Now, envision two parallel highways representing choices for Carlos. In one direction there is a series of negative reactions. He could quit, continue to be angry and resentful, look for another job, sabotage the employer and himself, and generally work out anger and frustration in ways that would be destructive. As an alternative, ask how Carlos can take control of a difficult situation.

On Monday morning Carlos asked the boss for fifteen minutes during the day to review his duties. The boss tried to put him off, but Carlos persisted. They set up a fifteen-minute time period in the afternoon. Carlos began by saying he was nervous and as a result had typed up some iPhone notes to prepare for what he wanted to say. He hoped the boss would excuse the use of his cellphone. The boss seemed slightly bored and eager to move on with the agenda. Though rattled, Carlos held firm.

He started by making a positive statement. "I really enjoyed this last week. I learned a lot and am excited about the future. I also realized that I haven't asked enough questions about the job. I didn't know about the overtime, and the excitement of working in this television station distracted me from the specifics of the job. I understand now that my job is not as glamorous as I thought it might be. But I would like to look forward to more challenging assignments. Could I spend an hour of my day copy editing in the newsroom? I know they need support, and I think that fits in with what you have told me about what the department does."

Carlos's boss actually seemed relieved. The suggestion was appropriate and not what he had expected. He had expected complaints about overtime, the menial position, or perhaps even threats, anger, and whining. Carlos was taking control of a small aspect of the job. He was asking for something that could lead to a goal without alienating the boss and losing the support of a valuable partner in this job. More importantly, Carlos felt in control. He felt that he had made up for his own mistake in not carefully evaluating the job and setting up expectations only to be disappointed. Carlos realized that the hour in the newsroom might not produce a new job, a promotion, or greater opportunities. But at that moment he felt empowered. He felt more in control and had the feeling of power.

In this story, Carlos has more to learn. He will have to be able to say no and to stand up for himself. He may learn to keep internal expectations in line with the reality around him. Most importantly, Carlos may ally with the boss to open up a line of communication and a partnership that may be invaluable in the future. Carlos controlled and influenced his boss while changing his personal perception of powerlessness.

Asking for Help

Lynnette is an executive assistant to a vice president in a large medical services corporation. Her primary job is to provide secretarial support to her boss. In addition she assists four other individuals who head up major projects and are mostly on the road. Three of the people work very well with Lynnette. The fourth, a relatively new marketing specialist, Don, frequently irritates her with interruptions, questions, and petty requests. She complained, "He is always asking me to do simple little things that he could more easily do himself."

Lynnette specifically focused on his need to have her fax and copy single pages. "It is more trouble for him to write out the instructions and put it on my desk than to just go and do it himself," she complained, adding angrily, "I can't just tell him to go and do it himself. You'd think he could figure it out. He's smart, he ought to know. Doesn't he realize I have other work to do?"

For Lynnette the clear answer was, "I'm okay, he's the problem!" The more she thought about how wrong Don was, the more resentful she became. As her anger began to occupy her thoughts and interfere with her work, Lynnette realized she needed help. She decided to talk with the Employee Assistance Program (EAP) specialist. Does your company have an EAP? If so, count yourself fortunate.

EAP programs are in effect worldwide and are now internationally accepted as a standard part of any benefit program. Most companies nationwide have EAP benefits and currently 97 percent of Fortune 500 companies have such programs available to employees. The EAP provides confidential assessment services to employees and family members whose personal problems negatively affect their work and wellbeing. The EAP interacts with the workplace, the employee, the community, and the employee assistance professional. Their trained specialists are required to adhere to a strict code of professional conduct and confidentiality. The EAP clinician is qualified to provide consultation, assessment, referral, and follow-up services agreed to by the work organization. Most EAPs are administered through the benefits and/or human resources department of a company. If a company does not have such a benefit, encourage the human resources director to look into providing an EAP for the employees and family members.

In addition, the EAP will refer employees and family members to the most cost-effective community resources, taking into consideration the nature and severity of the problem, treatment resources, and availability of healthcare benefit coverage. The EAP can also provide consultation to labor and management representatives on the constructive confrontation technique to help employees whose personal problems are affecting work performance and attendance. Don't wait for problems like Lynette or Carlos had. Take advantage of the services provided by the employee assistance program. Help will be invaluable.

Together, Lynnette and her clinician developed some steps to remedy the situation. He suggested she keep a record and then talk to Don. While Lynnette appreciated that he listened to her, the suggestion did not seem like a good one. She felt like he was putting her off. Now she had enemy number two.

In her next session, it was suggested that Lynnette confront the man directly. "Simply tell him how you feel." Lynnette lowered her eyes. "Well, I have never been very good at direct communication." The specialist answered, "Perhaps we could role-play?" They spent the next fifteen minutes rehearsing. Lynnette left the office feeling confident, and it seemed she would confront Don in a positive way, make some suggestions, and resolve the problem.

When Lynnette returned to the clinician's office the following week, she seemed renewed, even proud of herself. She had used what she had practiced, combined with a non-direct way of communicating her feelings. She had created something that was more comfortable for her. "I made a list of things I do to help him, and I made a list of things that he could do to help me. I presented it to him in terms of being partners. I said there were some things he could do to make my job easier and asked him if there was anything I could do for him that I wasn't currently doing. I handed him my list and he looked it over. He looked up smiling and praised me effusively. He said this list was really helpful and he would really pay attention to it and try to add ways that we could help each other. I was thrilled! I didn't have to speak to him directly, but somehow writing this down worked."

Indeed it did. Lynnette had taken control and created the impression she was doing more for him when in reality she was going to be doing less. She had taken control over the part of the relationship that she could influence. She had eliminated a hostile situation and felt empowered. Finally, she had allied herself in empowering him. A partnership was created by this constructive confrontation.

Serrila and Lynnette are examples of employees who have taken very big steps, steps that might seem small steps to the reader. They have both exhibited a good focus on the things that they can control. The greatest improvement concerns attitude. As an employee develops a greater sense of control over outward events, a growing sense of inner control will replace stress. As stress is reduced, symptoms of anxiety, depression, fatigue, and sleeplessness will be reduced.

Empowerment refers to giving to oneself the control and authority more often given to others. Each of these achievements involves an aspect of empowerment:

- Letting go of limiting beliefs.
- Increasing inner resources and self-confidence.
- Directing creative energies to what you really want.
- Transforming behavior patterns from self-defeating to self-creating.
- Moving from problem solving to vision creating.

Empowerment creates a strong and positive change in perspective. Thus, our perception of reality can be dramatically altered.

The opposite of empowerment is *depowerment*. This condition is characterized by blaming, negativity, fear, and confusion.

EMPOWERING CHECKLIST

Rate yourself on each pair of the characteristics below on a scale of 1 to 10, 10 being on the empowering side, and 1 being on the depowering side. Read each pair in Figure 1, and rate yourself by filling the blank with a number which corresponds to your feelings about that characteristic. For instance, if I am a big risk taker, a gambler, I might give myself a 9 on number 2. If I take very few risks in my life and always go with the sure thing, I might rate myself a 3 on number 2.

---

figure 1

EMPOWERING CHARACTERISTICS   DEPOWERING CHARACTERISTICS

‹ 10	9	8	7	6	5	4	3	2	1 ›

I display confidence. ____ I display little confidence.

I take risks. ____ I play it safe.

I take responsibility. ____ I am a victim.

I take action. ____ I am reactive.

I have tenacity. ____ I give up.

I am "power-on"/enthusiastic. ____ I am "shut down/low energy."

I am solution oriented. ____ I am problem oriented.

I am willing to be wrong. ____ I must be right.

I can handle change. ____ I am addicted to security.

I examine without judgement. ____ I complain without examination.

I am goal oriented. ____ I am in confusion.

I participate. ____ I withdraw.

I am flexible. ____ I am rigid.

I play a "bigger game." ____ I am stuck on a plateau.

I face fear. ____ I am fear-dominated.

I continue my growth. ____ I am staying in this place.

I show my humanness. ____ I don't need anyone.

I am receptive to new ideas. ____ I am narrow-minded.

I am accepting. ____ I am judgemental.

I am creative. ____ I am not creative.

I am self-directed. ____ I am floundering.

I am flowing. ____ I am resisting.

I am willing to change. ____ I must be right.

I keep my agreements. ____ I break my agreements.

I live in the present. ____ live in the past or future.

____

TOTAL SCORE

Now total your score by adding all the numbers. A perfect empowerment score is 250. If you score 175 or above, you are above average in power and confidence. If you score between 174 and 125, you are more average and able to handle most challenges. If you score below 125, you are a person who feels depowered. You lack confidence and are given to victim postures—blaming, negativity, and fear. It's time to set goals for self-improvement.

Look at the positive and negative traits you have checked; begin to develop goals for behavior change. The following questions will help you begin the plan for change. The questions are carefully selected from research and case studies. Resist the temptation to lightly skip over questions that may seem unimportant; be assured that each one will have a definite impact on your results. Read over all the questions first, then go back and carefully consider each one before answering.

1. What are some of the behavior changes I would like to make? For example, have I identified my next step up in the company? Do I work toward vision and goals? Am I able to set limits and assert my own needs? Do I like how I interact with my boss and coworkers?
2. Which behavior of those I have rated on the scale, or identified in question one, affects me the most now? For example, I am addicted to security, and that affects my ability to move up in the company. I am too fond of my niche.
3. How do I think my life will be different once I change?
4. Who and what do I think is holding me back? For example: My belief system holds me back. My fear of change, also.
5. Do I have the right to make any change I desire?
6. Which of the changes am I willing to tackle?
7. Am I ready to begin today?
8. Am I using the past as an excuse to stay where I am?

Having assessed your empowering traits, depowering characteristics, and having developed the basic outline for behavior change, you are now ready for the next step.

Water the seeds, not the weeds. The plan for behavior change should focus on positive aspects to reach, rather than negative traits to reduce. Think in these terms:

Focus on:	Rather than:
Increasing self-responsibility	Reducing victim status
Developing self-esteem	Reducing self-deprecation
Encouraging trust and risk-taking	Reducing fear and blame
Cultivating a positive attitude	Releasing negative expectations

Give yourself time, but start now.

Bloom Where You're Planted

In his internationally successful book *Megatrends,* John Naisbitt makes an interesting comment on roles in the workplace. He states, "What is called for is nothing less than all of us reconceptualizing our roles." If employees conceptualize themselves as powerless, their roles more like pawns than players, they will indeed feel the powerlessness, the resentment, and the frustration that comes with such a role. If, on the other hand, people perceive themselves as able to take control of small things, to influence decisions, to change perceptions, then they begin the process of empowerment.

Naisbitt speaks in global terms, examining large corporate empires. The principles are the same for those of us at mini, not mega, levels of power. Empowerment is a tool to increase the ability to become generals rather than foot-soldiers.

Develop your own definition of control relating to your job. To help you along, recall Serrila's story. Serrila had defined control as being made a permanent employee. With help she began to redefine control in terms of those things that she could directly influence. She started with her wardrobe and exercise. As a result, she gained control over her emotions, her anxiety and her fear.

Carlos had thought that landing the job meant control. Giving up his illusion of control, he learned that he could influence his boss through cooperation and partnership. Thus, he felt in control.

If we continue with Carlos and Serrila, the next step would be a pat on the back. Do this for yourself now. Celebrate your accomplishment. Simply reading this book, interacting with the exercises, and being willing to look at your part in difficult situations, in the workplace as well as outside, are great beginnings. Acknowledge yourself for taking time to examine your life, your work, and your future. Be ready to turn that internal victory into workplace success.

Take It Back

Recognize

1. List three situations you have experienced recently in which you felt a lack of control. (Examples: "I was asked to work overtime and couldn't say no," or "I wanted help but didn't ask for it.")
2. Now recognize one or more areas that affect your job where you perceive your boss has no control. (Examples: salaries, benefits, vacation policy.)

Respond

1. For each of the situations listed above, put down some empowering responses over which you do have control. (Examples: "I can't tonight, but tomorrow I'm available if you still need me.") List people who might role-play with you and ask them for help.

Reinforce

1. To further develop your confidence and skills for empowerment and change, move to the Reinforce step of Take It Back. In this chapter, we'd like you to evaluate your capacity to change. Complete the following inventory on coping with change.

Capacity for Change

Take at least twenty minutes to complete the exercise in Figure 2 by yourself, or to make the exercise even more effective, discuss the examples with your significant other or a close friend. Better yet, complete the exercise alone and then ask another to rate you. How do the responses differ?

In the past, whether you were aware of it or not at the time, every change you have gone through has been a process that (a) you handled well or felt in control of, (b) you handled adequately or felt somewhat in control of, or (c) you handled poorly or felt you had no control over. As you complete the items on Figure 2, visualize experiences from the past, and rate yourself on how well you feel you have dealt with each of those changes.

figure 2

W=**WELL** (high control)   P=**POORLY** (little or no control)
A=**ADEQUATELY** (some control)   N/A=**NOT APPLICABLE** (did not encounter)

1.	Leaving home	W	A	P	N/A
2.	Suffering the loss of a loved one	W	A	P	N/A
3.	Changing jobs	W	A	P	N/A
4.	Gaining or losing weight	W	A	P	N/A
5.	A breakup in a relationship	W	A	P	N/A
6.	Entering a new relationship	W	A	P	N/A
7.	Moving to a new city	W	A	P	N/A
8.	Having children	W	A	P	N/A
9.	Being laid off or fired	W	A	P	N/A
10.	An increase in stress	W	A	P	N/A
11.	Having someone leave you	W	A	P	N/A
12.	Getting a promotion	W	A	P	N/A
13.	Taking on a major new responsibility	W	A	P	N/A
14.	Getting married	W	A	P	N/A
15.	Getting divorced	W	A	P	N/A
16.	Ending or changing a destructive relationship	W	A	P	N/A
17.	Starting a new career	W	A	P	N/A
18.	Graduating	W	A	P	N/A
19.	Learning an important new ability or skill	W	A	P	N/A
20.	Starting a new business	W	A	P	N/A
21.	Being sick or in the hospital	W	A	P	N/A
22.	Having to deal with alcohol or drugs (self)	W	A	P	N/A
23.	Having to deal with alcohol or drugs (other)	W	A	P	N/A
24.	Going to work instead of staying home	W	A	P	N/A
25.	Staying home instead of going to work	W	A	P	N/A
26.	An unexpected financial setback	W	A	P	N/A
27.	Having the kids leave home	W	A	P	N/A
28.	Going back to school as an adult	W	A	P	N/A
29.	Living with war or the fear of war	W	A	P	N/A
30.	A change in faith or religion	W	A	P	N/A
31.	A change in the number of people in your household	W	A	P	N/A
32.	Losing something of great importance to you	W	A	P	N/A
33.	An unexpected calamity or catastrophe	W	A	P	N/A
34.	A change in the health of someone close to you	W	A	P	N/A
35.	Achieving an important goal	W	A	P	N/A
36.	Setting an important new goal	W	A	P	N/A

TOTALS ___ ___ ___ ___

YOUR PATTERN OF DEALING WITH CHANGE

To determine your personal pattern of dealing with change, and to get a clear picture of where you stand now, add up your responses in each of the first three categories. Enter the totals below.

(1) Well
(2) Adequately
(3) Poorly

To learn more about your individual response, add your scores again on these items as grouped in Figure 3.

figure 3	W	A	P
TOTAL	___	___	___
FEELINGS AND FEARS #1, 4, 10, 21, 22, 28, and 29	___	___	___
RELATIONSHIPS #2, 5, 6, 11, 16, 23, and 36	___	___	___
WORK AND SCHOOL #3, 9, 12, 17, 18, 20, 24, and 27	___	___	___
CHALLENGES #7, 13, 19, 25, 32, 33, 34, 35, and 36	___	___	___
FAMILY #8, 14, 15, 26, 30, and 31	___	___	___

The weighting of these areas are around 20 percent each (14-25 percent). Do you see that one or two areas are easier or harder for you to handle when change affects them? For example, some people handle job and challenge better than relationships. By more discretely analyzing your responses, behaviors you wish to modify for the future become clearer.

THREE

KEEP YOUR FRIENDS CLOSE AND
YOUR BOSSES CLOSER

*"Once in a while there's wisdom in
recognizing that the Boss is."*
Malcolm Forbes

Your attitude and work performance are tailored to the habits of your boss. Do you work for Darth Vader or Yoda? Probably neither. More likely your boss is an average person who faces many of the same problems that you do. After all, the person that controls your daily activities and enforces policies and procedures is human too. The boss is never purely evil or purely good, no matter how much you may be compelled to label him or her as either type. Saddled with the responsibilities of making decisions, keeping work on track, and trying to please both the people up the chain of command as well as the employees below is your boss' juggling act. How can you expect to win if you don't know what makes the boss tick? Why does she behave the way she does and what's behind her decision making?

You may never have the desire to be the manager or CEO. But would you like your job to be less confusing and more satisfying? Would you like to know why your boss does what he or she does? Inform yourself about what the other side is up to. Your boss knows the answers to these questions. What would it be like to know:

1. Why do you work better as a team instead of alone?
2. Why management doesn't ask your opinion on how your department can be improved?
3. Who will be released first when downsizing occurs?

4. What the purpose of staggered work hours is?
5. What the real purpose of your evaluation form is?
6. What the reason for new policies on alcohol and drug problems in the workplace is?
7. What a "ten-year workforce protection" program is?

Where do you find the answers? Your first step would be to read your company's policy and procedures manual. If there isn't one you may suggest the company put one together. Volunteer to help. Go to the library and take out several books about management. There are hundreds available. Just start with a title that sounds interesting to you.

In most of these books you will find the plans management has in store for you. You'll find training guides, learn to determine workers' personality types, and find out ways to provide the best possible working conditions. Some of the most interesting subjects in management books are about communication. The information goes on, page after page, book after book. But if the books are really about you and your future, doesn't it make sense to read as many as possible?

Our research shows that employees who have a basic desire to learn more about their business environment really excel after attending management workshops, seminars, and lectures. There are hundreds available nationwide, and many are free or cost little. Do a quick search on local resources, such as online newspapers, to find where they are and attend them. Call the chamber of commerce in your city for dates, times, and costs. You may even be able to attend one or two with your boss if you are willing to ask.

Understanding Your Boss

Almost all seminars include some form of "Boss Typecasting." Let's do a new version, with an outline of six prominent management profiles and some pointers to help you interact with each type of boss.

The Steamroller

The Steamroller is the boss who frequently interrupts you. His motto seems to be, "Do what I say. And be seen but not heard." He gives orders and commands, doesn't listen, and expects you to read his mind. To make headway with his style you need to:

1. Stand your ground. You may have to jump at openings, and repeat, but don't back down.
2. Get his attention. Start with a positive statement. Ask for advice or input. Not "help."
3. Make an appointment and meet on his turf.
4. Be organized and logical, using facts.
5. Eliminate small talk and be brief. Cut to the chase. Don't tell a story.

Big Sister (or Brother)

Then there's the Big Sister. She wants to be your buddy, share personal stories about her family and social life. She may share office gossip but rejects your overtures to familiarity. She'll waste your time and then make demands. With her you need to:

1. Remind her of your priorities. Ask if she'd like to change work assignments.
2. Acknowledge her chitchat and change the subject back to work tasks. Keep a businesslike demeanor.
3. Don't ask personal questions. Rather, say, "How can I help you?"
4. Be flexible but maintain the structure of your workday. For example, the employee might say, "I do want to hear this story, and I have to leave in five minutes."

5. Focus on work issues. Continue to work when she approaches your desk.

The Workaholic

When your boss is a Workaholic, she expects you be one too and asks for "voluntary" overtime. She wants you to work beyond your job description. She has high expectations that are hard to live up to. To keep her from making you into a workaholic too, you'll have to:

1. Set up boundaries. Have prepared responses to requests for overtime and favors. For example, "I'd really like to help you but that won't work for me."
2. Work at your own pace. Smile and say, "No."
3. Refuse to be intimidated.
4. Clarify your specific duties and hours with your boss. Perhaps you need to rewrite your job description for her approval.
5. Be patient and don't let the workaholic's habits become yours.

The Flake

Then there's The Flake, the absentminded boss. He forgets things, loses files, and papers, and can't remember what directions were given so contradictions are frequent. Like the Steamroller, he expects you to read minds. You need to:

1. Acknowledge by repeating the directions.
2. Ask specific questions and set deadlines, even daily times, for completion. "I can start that on Tuesday after 2:00 P.M."
3. Make extra copies of memos.
4. Make a note of all directions.

5. Be clear on your area of responsibilities. A current job description and daily goals can help.

The Shadow

When your boss is The Shadow, you'll rarely see her. She disappears and expects you to do everything. She offers few guidelines, and you may not know what is expected of you. You're always guessing, yet you are still held responsible. And she may even make you the scapegoat. You need to:

1. Arrange regular meetings. Keep rescheduling if she cancels.
2. Ask for directions and leave written questions, if necessary.
3. Don't assume and don't cover for her with others.
4. Pin her down as to time of return and what to tell callers.
5. Write it down!

The Wild Card

When your boss is The Wild Card, he says little and seems evasive. He seldom allows any feelings to show and seems aloof, but is probably shy and insecure. With him you must:

1. Ask open-ended questions.
2. Wait calmly for his reply. Don't fill the silence.
3. Avoid rushing.
4. Don't take his lack of communication personally. Plan enough time to wait.

Dealing with the Steamroller

Aaron explains his experience when he became the unsuspecting victim of a Steamroller's management style: "I was hired as a revenue officer for the Federal Bureau of Investigation in Fresno, California. During my first five years I received numerous special opportunities including being appointed manager in San Francisco. Four years later, I was promoted to a group manager position in Denver, Colorado. During my career with the FBI, I have received many Special Act and Superior Performance awards, including the coveted Outstanding Manager award. I have found my years with the service to be both demanding and rewarding. I say this to explain that I'm both experienced and fairly successful. Yet I was never immune to boss dilemmas.

"Undoubtedly, my most difficult time as a manager was while I worked for Barbara. Barbara was a few years younger than me. She was my division chief and managed six group managers, like I did. At the time she became my boss, I had already established myself as a respected frontline manager. I was supportive of my employees and succeeded in promoting several of them into management. On the other hand, I didn't hesitate to pursue performance problems when appropriate. Before Barbara's arrival, I had taken on several hard-core problems in the office but still maintained the respect of the employees. My group's productivity and quality of work was always equal to or better than the norm. I had received performance awards each year.

"In the face of all this, Barbara seemed intent on waging war with me. As my division chief, she was my immediate supervisor. She was openly hostile to me, critical of most everything I did. In her reviews of my group, she focused on the few deficiencies, while ignoring the positive aspects. It's very easy to find the problem areas if that's all you're looking for. She emphasized the substandard work being done by one of my employees without recognizing my efforts to correct the problem. Barbara belittled me and seemed to relish in being my superior. She made sure I knew who was the boss. I recall once we were trying to coordinate a meeting, and I suggested to Barbara that she tell me where she was going to be on a certain day so I could contact her. She literally shouted at me, 'I'll be damned if I'm going to tell some group manager where I am going to be!'

"Barbara continued her efforts to take shots at me. In one of her discussions, she told me I should just 'cut my losses' by stepping down from management. My attempts to dissuade her were ignored. I took my case to her boss, the chief. I pointed out how unreasonable and inconsistent Barbara had been. He listened patiently, but not surprisingly, backed Barbara.

"Barbara suffered severe mood swings," Aaron continued. "She could be pleasant on occasion but was a real bitch most other times. It seemed Barbara had to prove she was better than everyone else, especially men. She frequently held discussions standing in front of my desk, instead of sitting at my level. I believe she thought talking down to me would give her some sort of edge in life. After months of her act, Barbara began to wear me down physically and mentally. My self-confidence was undermined, and I began to question my own abilities. I felt powerless. To make things worse, the employee union somehow got a copy of the proposed management removal letter. Word quickly got around that I was about to be discharged despite my valiant efforts. I was embarrassed and humiliated. I considered legal action against the union.

"Fortunately, I received tremendous support from my family, particularly my wife. She helped me through the crisis. Without her, I would have been mentally crippled from the experience. Eventually I transferred to another division. I did the only thing I could have. I bowed out of Barbara's unnecessary battle, and kept her from destroying me. I look back on this experience and wonder, how did someone like Barbara ever get into such a position of power? I heard later that she had a somewhat checkered career before becoming a division chief. Just how did she get advanced to middle management? I still ponder this question."

After his transfer, Aaron went on to reestablish his reputation. Two years later, he was again selected as Outstanding Manager of his division and was subsequently promoted to division chief. The Steamroller had not been successful in her attempts to destroy Aaron. He rose above her onslaught, made a positive choice, and succeeded. He did not seek revenge. He knew who and what his challenges were and responded in a professional manner. At times, we must dodge the battle just enough until there's room to make a full escape.

FOLLOWING THE SHADOW

Terri had been the office manager in charge of 33 employees for several years. Mr. Angelo was the owner and out of the office most of the time. He always seemed to be with clients, either at their sites or entertaining them at lunch or dinner.

This boss was the Shadow. Terri enjoyed her job but wished Mr. Angelo would come in more often or at least keep in contact with her during the day. She never knew when he would show up. When he did, his voice came through the door before he did. "Where is everybody? What do I pay you people for? Terri!" he shouted, "Get me the Kincaid plans in my office, now!" She hurried to his office and handed him the file. "These aren't the plans I wanted! Can't you do anything right? I told you last week I would need the updated printout." Terri knew he had not told her about the plans, but said nothing. "Get the design team in here now! We're going to have a little chat."

The team filed into Mr. Angelo's office. After they were seated Mr. Angelo stood up and began to pace. "You people have let me down again. Why can't you get it together? You have had a week to come up with the Kincaid plans."

A wave of protest came from the team. "We didn't know. Nobody even told us!"

"Terri," Angelo said, "how could you slip up like this? You've made a costly mistake."

Good Lord, he's done it again, Terri thought. *He goofs up and I'm the scapegoat.* Terri glanced around the room. The team stared at her. Some shuffled their feet. She heard herself say, "I'm sorry, I must have forgotten."

After the meeting Terri went to Mr. Angelo's office. It was time for a talk. First she explained how much she enjoyed working for the company. Then she told him she would no longer take the blame for something she didn't do and that she would like to meet with him weekly. She asked that he also provide her with a to-do list instead of verbal communication. Terri felt good when she left the office. It was a start. Mr. Angelo was not a bad person, but as a boss he did need to come out of the shadows. Terri was wise enough to know that it's the act, not the person, which is deplorable.

Understanding the Workaholic

Frankie is an entrepreneur, the owner and operator of a small manufacturing company. He has an extraordinary need for control. He came up the hard way, with a limited formal education. He is self-taught and proud of it. At 41 years old, he is in great physical shape, swimming daily in his pool and working out in his home gym. And his biggest hobby, his company, is his baby. He is an enthusiastic people person with enough desire and ambition to make up for his lack of schooling.

It is well known that Frankie can charm the socks off the toughest customer. He's the kind of guy that could sell water to a well. Customers would come in complaining and leave laughing at one of Frankie's stories. But Frankie also can create a lot of confusion around him that is unsettling for his employees. He finds himself outdistancing the others, always pushing. The further ahead he gets, the greater his efforts to pull his team along. He even makes the assertion that they're holding him back. Frankie's solution to his problem is to harass, bully, cajole, flatter, and yell—whatever it takes to keep his "baby" moving.

Frankie brings in last-minute orders on a regular basis and demands his employees work excessive overtime to meet unrealistic deadlines. He wants to be involved everywhere, from the mailroom to the art department to the warehouse. He's often countermanding the foreman's orders to the crew. He creates havoc—changes plans that have been in the works for months, and then expects employees to work on their day off to bring the project up to speed. When one of his warehouse workers recently asked if he could go home after a twelve-hour shift, Frankie humiliated him by saying, "Can't take the heat, can you? Maybe I should hire a couple of cheerleaders to take your place." Frankie likes to take advantage of such a situation to tell his story to the workers. Did they know he slept only four hours at night? Did they know that he spent most of the night on the phone with his suppliers in Ireland and that he built this company from nothing, with financial support from no one? Frankie can work seven days a week for several months, then fly around to visit his suppliers. But only his body leaves the office. All day the overseas calls are forwarded to his phone. He is addicted to his job.

A young receptionist went to him once saying she couldn't work late because she had a class to attend. He fired her. She left in tears. Frankie called her the next day and rehired her. When she returned to work, there were two dozen roses on her desk. She went to the office and thanked him. He responded by telling her she had to get with it, that hard work was good for her and would make her sharp. Frankie alluded that there would be some hefty Christmas bonuses this year for people who went the extra mile.

It is typical of Frankie to attack his workers with unreasonable demands one minute and reward them the next. Once, after a particularly rough staff meeting filled with name-calling and blame, Frankie invited the entire staff to dinner at a very expensive restaurant, and he picked up the tab. At the dinner he was charming, laughing, making jokes. All the anger and frustration melted away as he told them what a great team they were. He told them that they would be stockholders when the company went public. Frankie was a dynamo dream-spinner. But the entire time he was speaking with them, his cell phone was in hand. Frankie never stopped. The next day his habits started right back up again.

As you might imagine, this company experiences high turnover. Within one year, three sales managers quit. Over a dozen warehouse workers and office personnel were either terminated or also quit. The remainder of the crew discussed setting up a meeting with Frankie. They liked him, in spite of his addiction, and could see the damage Frankie was causing. Frankie set the meeting time at six in the morning, as he often did. The group had invited a special guest to join them. It was Mr. Lopez, a member of the board of directors for the company, who would act as spokesman for the employees. Frankie commented that it looked "like an intervention."

"Well, it isn't a lynch mob," said Mr. Lopez. "Our purpose this morning is to create a win-win situation. Frankie, your employees like you. They are experienced, bright people who want this company to succeed. We are all of the opinion that you have the earmarks of a workaholic, and that's fine . . . for you. We are not asking that you change who you are. What we do ask is that you don't ask us to be the same."

Frankie interrupted, "I don't understand what all the resistance is about. Can't they just follow orders and do the job? That's what I pay them for. They need to rev up their production and make fewer mistakes. I have to see that they do. Business is business. If this company goes down there won't be any jobs to gripe about."

Mr. Lopez heard him out. "Frankie, we are aware that you own this company, you are the boss, and you call the shots. The difficulty is the manner in which you behave. In other words, it's not what you say; it's how you say it. You also have a tremendous amount of energy. Physically, most of us do not have your drive. Your sole focus is on the company and taking it to the top. That's okay. On the other side, you have employees with families; they deserve to spend time with them. You have young mothers who must pick up their children from sitters after work. They have a life outside of the company."

Frankie replied, "I try to give you people a good place to work. Look at some of the great parties we've had. I also pay a hell of a lot of money for your healthcare benefits." Frankie's feelings were hurt. Mr. Lopez said to think about some possible solutions before the next meeting.

During the following week, Frankie stayed out of the building. Mr. Lopez was in charge. It was a breath of fresh air. The work was done, and with few mistakes. But what's more, there was no yelling, no panic. The employees missed Frankie's motivation and humor, but not his aggressive style. The next meeting had a different tone. Frankie was his smiling self and Mr. Lopez smiled too. The announcement made by Frankie was a shocker.

"Look folks, I told you that I'm not going to change. I like to be on the fast track and see results. That's who I am. I see the vision, and it has upset me that you people don't. This is my decision, based on Mr. Lopez advice. I'm bringing in a business psychologist to work with all of us. Mr. Lopez tells me they have been of great benefit to many companies and the results are often positive. We'll see." The employees had stood their ground with Frankie; they intervened, and didn't allow themselves to be intimidated.

REDISCOVER THE JOY IN THE JOB

Make a list of things in your job that give you (or used to give you) joy, satisfaction, happiness, or elation. Visualize specifics and reflect on the tasks for a moment. Now, create your own affirmations and write, recite, and read them daily with feeling. Affirmations spoken in a hopeless or sarcastic tone are less effective than those issued forth with meaning and truth.

Replace
My boss is so disorganized.
My boss is grouchy.
My boss ignores me.
My boss won't give me a raise.
My boss hates me.
My boss picks on me.

With
My boss is extremely efficient.
My boss likes to joke around. I can encourage this behavior by smiling.
My boss is a busy man. He takes time for me if I need it, and I can learn to speak up.
My boss is reasonable. If I prove myself, I will be rewarded.
My boss doesn't know me well. If I take time to let her know me, intimacy will come.
My boss is detail-oriented. I can learn from her to be more precise and accurate.

By placing the behaviors in a different context you can put a different frame on the picture at hand. You can focus your energies more on yourself, instead of a battle that just increases time spent on blaming and procrastination. Who knows? You might even be able to learn something from your boss.

Establishing a Perimeter

One point must be made about the line between setting boundaries and taking abuse. If your employer is being verbally abusive or harassing you in any way, you should immediately contact your EAP representative or human resources department. They will help you assess an abusive situation. Even though the boss's behavior may have been tolerated by others, there are channels and procedures to support you.

Jean had just taken a new job as support secretary for a real estate firm. She quickly realized that her main boss was out in the field most of the time and was unavailable to her when he was in town. As the only support for nine sales reps, she found herself swamped with unreasonable demands, rude behavior, and frequent requests that stole her lunch hour and required overtime. Jean realized that the person who had previously occupied the position had obviously set very few boundaries, created no structure, and was pretty much a doormat for the group of agents who considered her their caretaker.

Without any clear guidelines from her boss, Jean felt she was on her own. She researched setting boundaries by reading some books on codependency. Slowly she started establishing boundaries on the job. She sent out a memo letting the agents know that sell sheets needed for weekend open houses would have to be submitted by 3 P.M. on Thursday. She attached an easy-to-use form she had created, which simplified the process and made clear what she needed. This solved the problem of last-minute Friday deadlines and having to stay late to make copies. She was fairly lenient during the grace period as the agents became used to her new system, but she eventually let certain agents know that they could make their own copies if they turned in their material late.

She began to create structure around the office, which made her boss happier, her coworkers happier, and pleased her. The office began to seem less hurried, less hectic, and less like a battleground. As a fringe benefit, Jean later asked her boss if the company would pay for her to go to school for a real estate license. He agreed to subsidize her classes at a community college and to pay for her test. When she received a license, her value to the company increased greatly.

Jean learned to set a perimeter, and get what she could out of her job. She was willing to devote some time and effort into turning the position around. You can turn your position around, too. Make your job what you want it to be. Don't be afraid to ask for what you want, especially in the way of marginal, or fringe, benefits. This could include, for example, a bonus for a special project that increases revenue, or compensatory time for working long hours or holidays. Remind yourself of those fringe benefits that can add value to your job when problems do arise.

Jean supported more than one boss. And in this age of cutbacks, layoffs, and downsizing, many of us will be providing the same support for multiple bosses, or even an entire department or company. You may get along fine with most of the people you work with, but sometimes there is that one person you simply don't mesh with. If that person is a boss or manager, it becomes more difficult. Be it a personality conflict or differences in work style, you don't like her, and she doesn't like you.

There are some strategies for working with that one person you can't get along with. Keep a log of all communications with that individual. Quite often miscommunications can be the source of interpersonal difficulties, and clearing the lines can solve that problem. Get clear with this person and stay that way. When asked to do something, restate the request as you understand it: "So, you are asking me to call John back to confirm your appointment?" Make sure you are clear. Vagueness and uncertainty will only work in someone else's favor, and it's never yours. When you are clear, you are in control. When you are unclear or are given unclear directions, you forfeit the battle. Admitting you don't understand helps you to regain control of a situation. Call the person back if you need to say, "I'm really not clear on what it is you wanted me to do here. Could you please clarify this?"

Almost every boss has good traits. I hope you can find some in yours. But every boss surely has some bad traits. And on many days these traits seem to overshadow the good ones. With human behavior as complicated as it is, and business pressures what they are today, this part of work is inevitable. No boss, no job, can be perfect—but if you fight the battles that arise from bad bosses and tough jobs wisely, you can be the perfect employee.

The characteristics and behaviors we've profiled above may be subtle in your boss. Look for similarities and ignore the differences so you can focus on action steps. Or maybe you've found others we've barely touched on. The value is in the discovery. So do your homework. Get to know your company, the ownership philosophy, and the personnel dynamics. Keep your eyes and ears open. Be objective. Once you know the enemy, peace is possible. At least you'll know enough to cope, and you just may become a better businessperson.

Take It Back

Recognize

1. Review everything you feel your boss (management) has done to harm you.
2. Make a list of all the things you feel you do for your boss that go unrecognized.
3. Consider how you feel when the boss reprimands, corrects, ignores you. Do you feel angry, petulant, or self-righteous? Be specific about your feelings.

Respond

1. What value do I receive from making the boss wrong? (e.g., I'm good and the boss is bad.)
2. What is my payoff for telling my problems to friends and coworkers? (Sympathy, understanding, attention, etc.)
3. Am I willing to look at my work in a fresh, more positive way? Have I ever done the same thing my boss is doing? Did anyone give me a break?

4. Are all my facts accurate concerning the boss's alleged wrongdoing?

Reinforce

Repeat the following:

1. I chose this job and take responsibility for it.
2. I encourage myself to laugh and see the humor in each day.
3. I reward myself when I deal well with difficulty on the job by_____.

And remember to keep the following in mind when feeling overwhelmed:

1. Focus on the task at hand, breathe deeply for a few minutes, and get a drink of water.
2. Forget about counting to ten. Count to one thousand before saying anything that could make matters worse.
3. Have a forgiving view of people. Believe that most people are doing the best they can.

FOUR

PERSONALITY PARTNERSHIP

"Knowledge is power." Whoever first said that phrase is right up there with the guy who invented Post-its. The statement is a part of everyday speech. It is an unarguable reality. And yet we often fail to use the route of learning for gaining power. But, you say, "I know my job very well. I have been doing it for a long time. In fact, I have created much of the job that I do." Knowledge of the job alone is not enough.

Our problems are created by our personal interactions with people. When a machine breaks down we experience an inconvenience. But it is the associated reactions of the people affected by the breakdown that exacerbate the problem. The machine can be fixed, but harsh words and hurt feelings are generated by people. The memories of anger and hurt continue to impair relationships. Thus, knowledge about work style personalities is an important tool for self-empowerment. Learning to better communicate with different personalities is a critical part of success in the workplace.

Mae-lin, a young, dedicated Certified Public Accountant, worked for a large accounting firm. She had two promotions in her first year on the job, and over the four years she worked for the company, she developed a reputation for attention to detail, flawless work, reliability, and precision. Her problems at work began when she received a promotion to the position of manager of the auditing department. Now she was not only responsible for others but also had a new boss. As department manager she came under the supervision of Dennis, who immediately found fault with her. It seemed everything she did was wrong in his eyes. He was annoyed by the amount of time she took to produce reports. He felt she should delegate more responsibility now that she was a manager. He told her that she did not communicate well in senior staff meetings.

Mae-lin tried to listen and incorporate Dennis's comments into her work style, but she was afraid to delegate, and when she did so she invariably found errors in the work of her subordinates. Nobody, it seemed, could match the high quality of work that she performed. Mae-lin became more and more frustrated and began, for the first time in four years, to feel inadequate in her job. She felt frustrated by her inability to communicate her problems to Dennis. She also resented that she had received no praise from him, no acknowledgment for the many correct things she was doing. She thought of quitting her job, but such an idea created more problems than it solved. Besides, she disliked change. The thought of looking for a new job and all the attendant problems frightened her. She began to experience sleeplessness, anxiety, fatigue, and other signs of depression. Finally she sought the help of an employee assistance specialist.

Mae-lin was experiencing a crisis in the workplace. Examining work style personalities could provide a solution. Her work style personality was characterized by precision, attention to detail, and follow-through. With her promotion to manager, however, something different was required of her. Specifically, she was asked to pay less attention to detail, to be more outgoing and communicative, to lead the team rather than be merely a team player—all characteristics of a more gregarious personality type. She was also experiencing a supervisor with a different work style personality than her own. Neither Mae-lin nor her supervisor could perceive their differences in terms of personality, but we can. Let's take a closer look.

For Mae-lin, organization, analysis, perfectionism, and thoroughness were part of the guiding principles of her life. Such a personality type does well with data and technical detail, which accounted for much of her success in the accounting profession. Mae-lin was also a loyal employee and very hardworking. But her personality needed support in other areas. She was not a natural leader. She had a tendency to be inflexible and get bogged down by details. She was not good at seeing the big picture or making quick decisions. Until her promotion, all of these missing or negative characteristics had not been a problem. However, as a manager she was required to exhibit more leadership, delegate more work, and accept a style of work that was different from her own and that made her uncomfortable.

Meanwhile, Dennis exhibited his preferred personality style. He judged others by their ability to communicate, to see the big picture, to forego small details, and make quick decisions. He dominated situations in order to overcome obstacles. He expected behaviors like his own personal style in Mae-lin. On the other hand, he needed someone like Mae-lin who was thorough and concerned with detail. Dennis could have learned to appreciate her capacity for loyalty and hard work. But because he did not value some of her predominant characteristics, he overlooked those aspects of her personality that he did hold in high regard.

This doesn't mean that Mae-lin can't be a good supervisor. Mae-lin and the EAP specialist worked together to accommodate her comfort level and still meet the demands of her position as a manager. Mae-lin learned to prepare notes before each meeting and rehearsed some statements to make on agenda items. She assertively volunteered for committee assignments instead of waiting to be asked. As she spoke in these limited areas, she began to feel more confident and speak more freely.

And what about Dennis? Is he just an insensitive jerk? As Mae-lin changed the way she interacted with Dennis, he praised her comments in the meetings and complimented the email delegation system she had established. Both were modifying their preferred and automatic styles to accommodate the other. They were acting on a modified golden rule: "Do unto others as they want you to."

Actions determine personality. In Shakespearean terms, "A rose by any other name would smell as sweet." Even though it is helpful to categorize yours and others' personality, those labels must reflect actions. After all, each day your personality in the workplace determines much about what you think and feel and how you behave. It determines how you make decisions; it determines what things are threatening to you. It is a factor in each personal interaction.

Several years ago a friend, Patt, and I were contemplating a trip to Kenya. I was excited about the trip, looking forward to going out on safari, photography trips, and typical tourist pleasures, when suddenly it occurred to me that I might be in some physical danger from the animals. Of course, the closest I had been to a dangerous animal was on the back of a tame horse. As I mulled over the idea of whether or not I might be afraid, I mentioned my feelings to Patt. She laughed. I didn't understand why she found what I said so funny.

She smiled and said, "Oh, no. I know what you'll be afraid of."

"What?" I said. "I really want to know."

"*Boredom*," she replied. "You are afraid of being bored."

As a good friend of many years, Patt knew me very well. She was making an intuitive assessment of my work style personality, which I was taking on vacation. I was frightened, actually phobic, of being bored. And without knowing it, my fear of boredom had led me to make preparations for entertainment. I was making lists of books to take, packing crossword puzzles, planning touristy activities. In fact, I had planned to take office work along (I was going to keep all of this secret from my traveling companions for fear of their ridicule!). But my work style personality was pervasive. Boredom was my fear.

Each of us has a distinct work style personality. A few of us are aware of what that work style personality is, or intuitively make choices that reflect such awareness. We know well the conditions under which we work best. We try to make these conditions a reality. However, like Mae-lin, we find that conditions change and we must adapt and accommodate. We must get out of our comfort zone or we will eventually feel powerless and out of control.

Patt tells a story of personality literally on display in the workplace. "I recently walked into the data processing offices of a large insurance company where I had been asked to consult on marketing strategies. The large workroom had just been remodeled and the area was quiet, light, and very conducive to concentration. Each worker had an individual cubicle that was well soundproofed and padded, even though all were open. As I looked across the room I counted about 40 cubicles. The sound level was quiet and the environment was pleasant, though seeming to lack individuality. But then my vision was attracted to a few items that stuck up from the tops of the four-foot-tall open cubicles. Some employees had fixed small stuffed animals, cartoon caricatures, flowers, plastic figures, and other small objects on the top and sides of their cubicles. They identified their territory, but even more so their personalities.

"If you could have a bird's-eye view of these cubicles, you would see how each one reflected the employee's work style personality. Some had placed family pictures prominently throughout their cubicles. Pictures of babies, weddings, and themselves with celebrities or at parties dominated their workspaces. Others had very tidy and immaculate cubicles with no extra clutter on the work surfaces. Others showed humor, displaying cartoons, bumper stickers, and slogan buttons. Still others showed nurturing and caretaking aspects of personality with flowers, candy dishes, and potted plants. Seeing a philodendron tendril lovingly pinned so that it reached the top of the cubicle for as much sunshine as it could get, I thought, *work style personality in action.*"

To gain control and be empowered by your own personality, you must first understand its distinctive nature and learn for yourself how you are alike or different from others. There are many ways to learn more about personality. One way is to take a professionally administered individual personality test. Often these tests are used in hiring decisions, administered in training, or used with promotion. If you are interested in an in-depth assessment, talk to an EAP specialist, check with the human resources or training department, or look in the yellow pages for testing services. But for a first step, let's try something simple.

Take the test on Figure 4 to develop an understanding of your personality. People are different, but we are more alike than different. Each one of us is unique and special, yet we share many common personality patterns and styles. The DISC personality profile can help us understand our dominant work styles. The intent of this exercise is not to put you in a box or to stereotype you, but simply to provide an additional dimension of understanding. When you complete the exercise, follow the instructions at Figure 5 to determine which of the four personality types best describes you.

Evaluate Your Style

In Figure 4, check the word from either Column I or Column II that best answers the question, "If I were forced to choose, I would say I am . . ." Choose the one that applies 51 percent of the time or more. Then do the same for Column III and Column IV.

figure 4

	I			II	
	more animated	____	____	more passive	
	more a leader	____	____	more a follower	
	more assertive	____	____	more accepting	
	more challenging	____	____	more hesitant	
	more lively	____	____	more meditative	
	more confrontive	____	____	more supportive	
	more gregarious	____	____	more a listener	
	more a risk-taker	____	____	more cautious	
	more intense	____	____	more relaxed	
	more forceful	____	____	more tentative	
			____	TOTAL	

	III			IV	
	more flashy	____	____	more formal	
	more spontaneous	____	____	more disciplined	
	more responsive	____	____	more self-contained	
	more impulsive	____	____	more methodical	
	more intimate	____	____	more distant	
	more feeling	____	____	more analytical	
	more people-oriented	____	____	more task-oriented	
	more outgoing	____	____	more reserved	
	more dramatic	____	____	more matter-of-fact	
	more warm	____	____	more cool	
	TOTAL	____			

Now total the check marks in column II and put that score on the Total line. Circle the Total number on the horizontal line on Figure 5.

Also total the check marks in Column III. Circle the Total number on the vertical line on the graph. Draw a line through both circles to find where your personality lies on the scale.

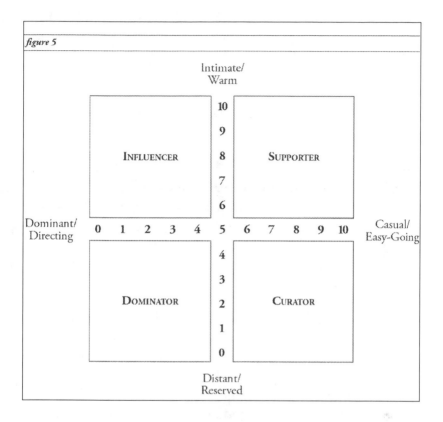

figure 5

THE DOMINATOR

Not only directing the play, this type wants to be the actor, producer, and critic. In the office hierarchy, they're the general. Dominators attempt to control and dictate.

They are decisive and direct. They get things done and are good at seeing the big picture, accomplishing goals, and overcoming obstacles. In the workplace their confidence and decision-making ability is an asset but may be mistaken for arrogance. They are good leaders, businesslike, and task-oriented. But for each type there is a shadow side. Dominators may become bullies, display insensitivity to needs unlike their own, alienate and intimidate others. Donald Trump, Robert DeNiro, Hilary Clinton, and Tiger Woods exhibited this personality style. John F. Kennedy displayed the classic leadership style of dominance coupled with a high level of the Influencer style.

The Influencer

Influencing, persuasive, and often talented at acting, this personality characterizes Steve Martin, Ellen DeGeneres, and Oprah Winfrey. They often strive to be the commander-in-chief of office politics. This personality type is warm, creative, charismatic, and energetic. Influencers talk a lot, entertain, tell jokes, and generally dominate a conversation. They like to be the center of attention and communicate well. They are people-oriented and usually optimistic. They value popularity and social recognition.

These qualities characterize their work and personal styles. Their value to an organization is obvious. In terms of work, the downside often includes a lack of follow-through, self-centeredness, reputation of "flake," and lack of attention to detail. They may fail to see the important points, letting their desire for social recognition and popularity take precedence.

The Supporter

Agreeable and personable, this type is caring, helpful, and definitely a team player. They like harmony, are very likable, loyal, and value security and belonging to a group. Michelle Obama, Michael J. Fox, and Nancy Reagan share these qualities. They are helpful, predictable, and patient. In the workplace, this style contributes to their success. Limitations may be seen in their wish not to take risks, their avoidance of constructive conflict, their inability to be critical or express negative feelings. When thwarted over time they may become resentful and engage in passive aggressive actions.

THE CURATOR

Attentive to detail and logically analytic, this type of personality is systematic, consistent, and accurate. Such personality types value facts, data, and are often seen as perfectionists. They like control, structure, the status quo, and accepted order. They are not known for their communication skills and may flee in the face of controversy, become silent or alternately autocratic and given to lecturing. Bill Gates and Diane Sawyer share these traits. In the workplace these qualities are very desirable, again, given the right position. Security and order are part of each workday for the precisionist. On the downside they can be stubborn, aloof, and boring. They often move slowly, resist change, and fail to express feelings, especially of a personal nature. They are uncomfortable with intimacy and emotion.

Your style—whether Dominating, Influencing, Supporting, or Curating—doesn't reflect all your qualities. Each of us has a bit of each style in our makeup. When angry the gentlest Supporter can act out his rage and throw tantrums. When pressed, the Influencer can make a budget and balance a checkbook. The idea is that we have a preferred or dominant style. These are the attributes that shape your personality most strongly. No personality is one-dimensional. For every person who enjoys being on stage, there is someone in the audience terrified of public speaking. For every person who defines a good job as one that lasts his or her entire working life, there is another person who changes careers with the seasons. There is no right or wrong, no good or bad, just differences.

Understanding our own personalities helps us to understand and accept the way others work and relate to us in the workplace. All of us harbor certain undeveloped, or perhaps secret, abilities within our list of attributes. We can often discover a larger number of possibilities for our working relationships than we might have suspected. As we begin to use better ways of communicating, we also learn more about others. They in turn reveal their secret abilities and offer more depth in a relationship than we might have anticipated. The people around us take on new dimensions. The working relationships grow and are more successful.

Success Is a System—Not Luck

Hank had consulted with us in his capacity as Director of Marketing for a large casino. He worked in Reno but flew all over the world finding new locations for sites and helping foreign countries establish their own casinos and tourist attractions. His description of the job provoked images of glamour, high rollers, straight shooters, and stacks and stacks of casino chips. Hank, however, was not immune to personality incompatibilities. The CFO, Mike, had one work style that proved to disagree with Hank's. Hank was handsome, six-foot-four, and fit perfectly into his black pinstripe Dolce & Gabbanna suit. He straightened his Thomas PINK "Eldredge" knot tie and flashed his Cartier watch as his French cuffs slid up. He gestured broadly, saying, "Mike simply doesn't understand what marketing is. He doesn't get that you have to spend money to attract these people. He constantly questions my expense account and budgets. He doesn't understand that these high rollers expect to live a first class lifestyle. They expect to be taken to lunch. They expect the limousines to pick them up. They expect a personal attendant at their sides." Hank became more agitated as he waved his arms and talked faster. "He's always bugging me about petty details. I can't get my budgets approved without him going over it with a fine-toothed comb. He makes me justify everything." When I asked what Hank had tried in order to effect solutions, he responded, "I've tried everything! I've given him complimentary tickets to ball games and special seats for openings. I had his wife picked up in a limousine for a shopping trip with other VP wives. I have done everything. He doesn't want the tickets. He seems disappointed by all my efforts. I just don't know how to relate to him."

Because this was a workshop in work style personality I involved all the members of the group to provide a solution to Hank's problem. I had previously spoken about work style personalities and had identified each personality type. The group was asked to begin by identifying Hank's personality even though we knew it well. Hank is a commander-in-chief: entertaining, influential, and a born persuader. He is perfect as a salesperson—outgoing, entertaining, and likable. He is also a flashy dresser. Each week we could look forward to a new outfit that was both expensive and perfectly suited to him. Members of the group had no trouble in identifying Hank's personality, in reading him perfectly. Hank smiled as aspects of his personality were revealed, including negative ones—lack of attention to detail, not wanting to be confined by traditional standards, and judging others by action rather than thought. Hank knew that he had these limitations in his personality. He expected others to support him, to pick up the pieces where his work style personality lacked.

The group was then asked to paint a personality picture of Hank's nemesis, Mike, the chief financial officer. The group became animated, describing him as a man who wore brown suits, and when his suit coat was removed, he had a plastic pocket protector. He carried sharpened pencils and pens and had worked as an accountant before his promotion to CFO. In general, Mike was described as having an analytical, Curator style.

Hank was then asked to bring his chair into the center of our circle and to select from the people in the group the one who had the Curator work style of his nemesis, the person most like Mike. A little embarrassed, Hank pointed to Janet. She brought her chair to the center of the room. I asked the two of them to role-play how Hank would ask for an increase in his budget, and Janet's job was to act as her personality suggested.

Hank stood up and reentered the circle as if entering an office. He remained standing. "Hi there, Janet. I've got two tickets to the new show opening Saturday night at the Luxor. I thought you and your hubby might enjoy it. By the way, I need about a thousand more in my budget for the upcoming golf event. You know we've got some big spenders coming in, and you know they expect the best."

Janet just looked at Hank. Several moments elapsed before she responded. "Thank you," she said slowly, "for the tickets. Do you have a detailed proposal for the budget increase?"

"Oh, come on, Janet," Hank laughed, "You know me. You can fill in all those details. You know how much this stuff costs. What do you want from me?" Hank began to scribble some notes on a piece of paper taken from her desk. "Look, here are the items and here are the amounts we need to increase them by. Is that good enough?" Janet crossed her arms and said that she would take a look. The role-play ended.

Janet seemed to be angry. She was pulling away from Hank and seemed almost resentful of her position. When asked about her feelings, she laughed, "Yes, I did become angry and resentful. I really got into the role. The word that comes to mind for me is frivolous. I think Hank is frivolous. He doesn't understand the meaning of money. He doesn't have any respect for my job. He throws these tickets at me, yet he has never once asked me to do anything with him."

In such a brief, contrived moment Janet's personality was clearly in contrast and in conflict with Hank's. Hank sat very still. It seemed for the first time he had begun to see Mike as a person rather than an obstacle to his desires. I encouraged them to pursue the feelings that Mike and Janet might have had. The group validated the impression of anger and feeling discounted on Mike's part. We made several suggestions as to how Hank might improve his communication with the CFO regarding the budget.

Several weeks later Hank reported back to the group. He began by saying that on the day of his presentation to Mike he had picked out a very conservative suit. He even thought of buying a new shirt that didn't have French cuffs. Hank knocked before entering the CFO's office and immediately sat down in a chair. He had a pencil in his hand and a folder with him. He told the group how the CFO had noticed the folder and seemed very interested in it.

"This is characteristic of the analytic personality type," Janet said. "I don't take anyone seriously who comes into my office empty-handed. If the person doesn't have a pencil and a notebook, I feel that they aren't serious and won't remember what I say. So I just stop talking."

"Right!" Hank said. "That's just how it was." Hank went on to tell Mike that he was sorry the two of them hadn't gotten to know one another better. He told him, "I've got some tickets here for the UNLV basketball game. I was wondering if you'd like to go with me. Do you think your wife would let you go for a Saturday afternoon?"

The CFO's eyes had lit up. "I'd really like that."

Hank resisted the impulse to say, "I'll pick you up in a limo and we'll have a high time of it." He suggested they meet at the stadium after lunch instead. Hank then began to present a budget in a more organized way. His wife had even helped with the budget during the previous week. He said he had begun to notice that his wife and the CFO had many personality characteristics in common. The group speculated that Hank had married a woman who paid more attention to detail, was a loyal supporter, and was more comfortable as a team member than a quarterback. He agreed that his wife had given him valuable insights into the personality of the CFO.

PERSONALITY PARTNERSHIP

As a result of Janet's insights and the group's help, Hank and Mike had the beginnings of a new relationship, one based on personality partnership. They had become partners by complementing one another's work style personality. Each was now able to stop being defensive and move forward in a partnership. Hank now gave more acknowledgment to Mike for his important role in Hank's success. Mike felt validated. In his eyes Hank had become more responsible and serious. As a result he began to be less frugal, less demanding, and less critical of Hank's requests for money.

Nothing changed until there was a greater understanding of personality, of the individual's style and preferences. Hank began to understand Mike's personality and tried to meet his needs instead of insisting on his own while displaying an overpowering personality style. Mike responded in kind.

But isn't this manipulative? Wasn't Hank taking advantage of this conscientious, analytical type? Wasn't Hank using him and even making fun of him? Well, let's look at it another way. Let's view Hank as treating Mike in a way that the CFO desired to be treated. The CFO had been misinterpreting Hank's overtures and expected the tickets and the gestures to be followed by more personal offers of friendship. As Hank began to appreciate the differences in their personalities, they in fact became friendlier and thus better partners. Hank noticed that those things that he loved about his wife he disliked in the CFO. But he could understand that the love and intimacy that characterized his marriage could also serve as an example for overcoming problems in the workplace. He understood that getting closer to coworkers creates greater respect for their hidden attributes, secret talents that are the very positive nature of every personality.

Now, let's take a next step. How can you better work with and for those people who have work style personalities different from your own? Understanding personality can be one of the most valuable tools for success in the workplace. You may find that the different styles will make more sense to you if you attempt to fit family members and coworkers into the categories listed in Figure 6. Work with people who are close to you to test changes. Try new approaches to your usual way of relating.

Increasing Your PEP:
Personal Effectiveness with Personality

This chart provides tips for how you can improve communication with each personality type. When making requests, asking for help, or just improving everyday communication you may find these suggestions in Figure 6 helpful. Make your changes, and watch them change!

Understanding others is the key to meaningful relationships. But relationships, whether on the job or off, can be very hard and require effort. Accept that each person is doing her or his best to survive and get on with the job. Sometimes our attempts to cope are successful, but at other times we simply fail. We can be knocked over by life's pressures. No one is immune to being overwhelmed, stressed out, and emotionally exhausted. But personality education and the resultant personality partnering can be valuable resources for dealing with those hard knocks of life and work. Enhance your ability to effectively cope and build stronger relationships by using your personality assets, compensating for areas of difference, building on knowledge, and moving to action.

Take It Back

Recognize

1. You have evaluated your personality style. Did the instruments in this chapter assess you accurately? Is your personality work style an effective one for the job you have?
2. Notice how your personality strengths and weaknesses affect your interactions with others in the workplace. Do your workplace and your job mesh with your work style personality?

---

figure 6

For the **Dominator**

- Be clear, specific, brief, and to the point.
- Stick to business. Come prepared.
- Present the facts logically; plan your presentation *efficiently*.
- Provide alternatives and choices for the Dominator to consider when making a decision.
- Provide facts and figures about probability of success or effectiveness of options.
- Motivate and persuade by referring to how this fits in with his or her objectives.

For the **Influencer**

- Plan an interaction that supports the Influencer's dreams and intuitions.
- Use time to be stimulating. Allow for storytelling and entertainment.
- Don't deal with details verbally; put them in writing; pin them to modes of action and deadlines.
- Provide ideas for implementing action and assign responsibility for follow-up.
- Offer special, immediate, and extra incentives for the person's willingness to take risks.

For the **Supporter**

- Start (briefly) with personal chitchat. Break the ice.
- Show sincere interest in the Supporter as a person; comment on pictures on the desk.
- Be patient, listen, and be responsive.
- Present your case softly, nonthreateningly. Ask *how* questions to draw out the person's opinions.
- If you disagree, look for hurt feelings, personal reasons. Try to reassure.
- Define clearly (preferably in writing) individual contribution.

For the **Curator**

- Prepare your case in advance, in writing. Be accurate.
- Approach the Curator in a straightforward, direct way; stick to business, no chitchat.
- Build your credibility by listing pros and cons to any suggestion you make. Provide evidence.
- Present specifics and do what you say you can do. Take your time, but be persistent.
- Draw up a scheduled approach to implementing action with a step-by-step timetable; assure that there won't be surprises.
- Give time to verify reliability of your actions; be accurate, realistic.

3. Can you identify the personality type with which you work most effectively? Is that the style your boss and close coworkers have? If not, list some effects this has on you and your productivity. Reading this list you may see how some small changes can make a large difference.

Respond

1. Practice approaches to test personality style. For example, approach the desk of a Supporter and comment on the personal pictures on display. See how your overture is received. Does this interaction produce a positive result? Do you see a difference from previous interactions? This may suggest a new way to initiate communication with this individual.
2. List elements of your work style that you would like to change. For example, if you are an Influencer, would you like to be more organized? Would you like to pay more attention to detail? Set aside some time to devote to paperwork during the day. Make specific efforts to change.
3. Practice new greetings and approaches to individuals whose personality styles are often different from yours. You may want to rehearse with someone who has a similar style.

Reinforce

Practice these statements:

1. I now discover how wonderful I am. I accept myself and others just as we are.
2. I am open to new ideas. I release the old and welcome the new into my life and job.

3. It is easy for me to reprogram the computer of my mind. I accept new information about others.
4. I see with new eyes. I see others as they wish to be seen. I treat others as they wish to be treated.

To expand and reinforce your knowledge:

1. Look for online courses on personality through extension programs and community colleges. Make a commitment to learn more self-awareness.
2. Explore personality testing through the company-sponsored EAP or the mental health benefit of the healthcare plan.
3. Practice the "golden (personality) rule," *Do unto others as you want them to do unto you.*

FIVE

BATTLE TACTICS

No reader needs a book to document the day-to-day frustrations that accompany earning a living in America. We all know about that firsthand. Each of us reacts to those frustrations and conflicts.

But sadly, many people do so by trying to get even using sabotage, revenge, and even violence. Such behaviors rob us of money and good health, waste time, and disrupt productivity in the workplace.

Retaliation encourages the mentality of "me versus them." It is the first step in the process of blaming others, of neglecting the resources you have to solve problems and change conditions.

People who sabotage their companies are not necessarily bad employees, vandals, or drug addicts. They are usually ordinary people who have been yelled at one too many times by a boss in a bad mood or an unreasonable higher-up. They may be people who learned they were expendable after a lifetime of service; perhaps they are the first to have their salaries cut in a budget crunch. They are frequently extraordinary people kept to doing ordinary jobs. They see themselves as under attack, singled out, and targeted by others. They are people who have become disillusioned and unproductive for themselves and for others in the workplace. This kind of personal sabotage extracts a high cost, both from the workplace and from the employee.

SCANDAL IN THE WORKPLACE

In his book, *Sabotage in the American Workplace*, Martin Sprouse defined sabotage as "anything that you do at work that you are not supposed to do." Employees who commit sabotage are not necessarily chronic malcontents, who constantly question company policy, rules, and procedures; nor are they malingerers. They are frequently smiling, compliant, loyal employees, who quietly go about their jobs and rarely reveal the extent of their desire for revenge, the suppression of their anger, or the activities by which they sabotage both themselves and the company. Keith is an example of such a saboteur.

Keith describes his boss Sasha as "a sexist bitch." He talks a lot about reverse discrimination and says that Sasha is a power-hungry woman trying to get rid of him so she can replace him with a woman. "I can't say I hate the job," Keith says. "I like the people I work with. If I just had a different boss I could be really happy here."

Keith is a supply clerk. The job site is a large supply room, caged for security. One of his jobs is taking inventory, which he dislikes and does poorly. The accuracy of his counts has become a point of contention between himself and his supervisor. Sasha spot-checks his work, finds errors, and brings them to his attention. She accuses him of sloppiness, lack of attention, and inability to concentrate. She has given Keith an oral warning consistent with the company's personnel guidelines in order for him to correct these deficiencies.

Keith, in retaliation, began to steal from the inventory. Using a complicated system he created in the computer, Keith made it almost impossible for anyone to follow his moves. He later admitted that the items he took were not of much use to him, and most of them ended up in his garage. Keith also sabotaged equipment. He jammed new staplers and returned them to the box, scratched computer disks, emptied contents of new bottles and replaced the tops. Such petty sabotage brought an unknown and unseen havoc as well as a high price into the workplace. What if Keith had simply used a constructive technique to address his grievances? Let's look at some of his alternatives.

Suppose Keith had confronted his boss not with facts but simply with his views for a constructive confrontation. "I feel that you would rather have a woman working in this position.

I feel discounted and always picked on." What did Keith have to lose? He had already received an oral warning. He was very unhappy in his job, and he was anxious to leave the company.

Constructive confrontation is a positive way of bringing what bothers us to the attention of others. Too often confrontation is thought of as a fight or an argument, something negative and aggressive. In Keith's case, this confrontation could simply have been statements of feelings. His boss might have responded with ridicule and demeaning statements. Then Keith could have walked away. But the boss might have listened and tried to find better ways of working with Keith. Having been alerted to his feelings, she might have been more sensitive. In any event Keith would probably have felt better had he expressed his feelings and confronted his boss with what he perceived to be her unfair treatment of him.

In yet another scenario, perhaps his boss might have gained understanding about what Keith perceived as her prejudice. Sasha might have been able to reassure him of the fact that she didn't want to replace him in the job, that she valued certain aspects of his performance, but that she wanted some changes. Perhaps the two of them could have worked together to be more constructive and less confrontational. In this story, Keith was laying all the blame on his boss and taking no responsibility. She had sinned in his eyes, and he could not forgive her. The process of empowerment begins when we move past blaming and get on with the job.

Perhaps in yet another scenario he could have surrendered. Surrender is one of the simplest, and yet most complex, of all the many tools used to change behavior. It's both the safest and riskiest way, the easiest and most difficult step. For many of us, it is the most fear-producing and yet can be the most comforting. Surrender is a straightforward idea, yet it is often misconstrued. "How can surrender be good?" you ask. "Isn't it weak to surrender? Haven't I been surrendering all these years to bosses and authority? Look where that's gotten me. If I did go along with this surrender idea how is it done? What do I give up, and who do I give it to?"

Often old definitions of surrender paint a negative picture of weakness and defeat. It might seem like another word for giving up. Perhaps visions of western movies where the bad guys keep surrendering to the good guys appear. Maybe it is invading armies and the tattered white flag raised over a fort's broken walls. Surrender is associated with loss of control over our lives, with failure. We're taught champions never fail and they definitely never surrender. But they do. It's a surrender to win.

GIVING UP, NOT IN

Let's look at a dictionary definition of surrender, one that is frequently overlooked: ". . . to yield to the possession or power of another." Doesn't that really mean exchange? Look at common uses of surrender as an exchange: We surrender the title of our old car when we trade it in for a new one. The bank surrenders the promissory note we've signed when we pay off the debt. A defeated army surrenders in exchange for promises of protection and territory. Thinking of surrender as an exchange, not a defeat, may help us accept the concept more readily. It can also show us how to surrender. Surrender means exchanging the bad—our old ideas, our old point of view, our old rigidity—for a path that yields more rewards.

What if Keith had tried seeing things her way? "Well," he might say, "She's going to fire me anyway, but I'll try it her way for a while." He could have begun to work more methodically, more carefully. He could have invited her spot-checks, trying to see his work as she saw it.

In surrendering, we accept new ideas. Part of this exchange involves learning to trust ourselves and others. To do this, we first may need to sever ties with self-will and ego. Admitting our ways are not working is a kind of honesty we can use to open our minds and hearts and see the sources of our fear and anger. Now we are searching for and accepting new ways of behavior. By letting go of fear, anger, and resentment, we gain freedom, joy, and a sense of control. "I may not like this, but I've decided to do it."

You've Given Everything But Up

A good way to practice letting go of our fears and our need to control is simply to fake it until we make it. Perhaps Keith could have learned better work habits by surrendering his resentment and trying it Sasha's way. He might protest, "But aren't you asking me to make myself a doormat for these demanding bosses and corporate machines?" No! Submission is a counterfeit of surrender. We submit when, in our insecurity, we look for care from someone strong and protective. We submit to another's ideas and opinions, becoming sheep rather than shepherds. This is much easier than taking a deep, honest look at our lives and needed changes.

Only when we've done the groundwork and been willing to let go completely of our old resentments can we change. But how can we translate such a vague concept into something that has real meaning in our lives?

Easy Does It, But Do It

Here is a list of tools, ideas, and actions that can help us understand surrendering. Remember the goal is to create a better work situation for *you*.

Make a List

Take a piece of paper and make a list of what it is you feel or have been told you should change, or you feel are unreasonable demands. Keith might list:

Surrender	*In Exchange For*
My insistence on my style	More peace each day
My work habits	Less criticism from the boss
My stealing supplies	Feeling better about myself
My growing resentments	Pride at speaking my mind

The idea is to think in terms of not only giving but receiving. This may be hard to do at first as you fear that if you give up something, or ask for change, you will somehow become vulnerable. If you're not sure what to write, ask a coworker or friend for help.

Have a Wingman

There's a tool that is very effective in the fight against anger, fear, and resentment and that is speech. Sometimes the hardest things to surrender are our insecurity and pride. We still think it's weak to ask for help, that it's again waging the "me-against-the-world" war. Be honest. How many battles have we won with our "me, myself, and I" army? We all need help sometimes. We need someone to listen. We need another's perspective on the things we find troubling. And who better to listen, understand, and help us than someone who's just like us? Take a deep breath and ask for a coworker's perspective. Be willing to communicate. Be willing to accept the help others are waiting to offer.

Act As If

Sometimes we may identify something we know we need to surrender, but we can't seem to make the break. It's too important, or perhaps it's something we think only we can solve: "No one else really knows what I do. No one else sees the side of the boss that I do." We can continue to carry these chips on our shoulders or we can "act as if." Act as if we no longer needed to be right when we come into conflict with our boss.

Act as if we aren't angry when our boss schedules us to work on Saturday. Act as if we no longer feel guilty when we find a lost file that we had accused him of losing.

A look at Doreen's story will show us how to "act as if." She had been unwilling to surrender her pride. Doreen, an administrative associate, worked for Tim, who was a poor communicator. She made up for this by her attempt at mind reading. She tried to anticipate the needs of both the department and Tim. Her performance evaluations reflected his appreciation for her good work, but her position did not. Doreen got passed over for consideration for a newly created position as market analyst with a commensurate pay increase. She spoke to the human resources director asking for reasons. "Yes," replied Paulette the HR director, "You meet the qualifications, but Tim feels you aren't a real team player. He praises your initiative but feels you wouldn't do well working with a team that requires input to the analyst's concerns and synthesizing of their ideas."

Doreen was shocked and very angry. She decided to confront Tim. She was surprised at how attentively Tim, who sat quietly and met her gaze very directly, listened to her. When he began to speak, she had yet another shock. She realized her attempts to mind read had really been a rationalization for her own self-will and desire to do the job her way. She saw that when Tim did attempt to direct her efforts, she had brushed off his ideas and discounted his comments. She knew she would have to change.

"So I resolved to really listen, to be patient," she said. "Tim's way of speaking is very slow, and I was jumping in too soon. I was frustrated. At first it was hard for me. But you should see me now. I'm really a team player, no longer 'stuck in the trenches.'"

Doreen acted as if. She showed her resolve to change and learn from others. Soon the acting (that she felt like listening to people) became the real thing. Feeling a part of a team began to feel natural.

Assess Your Teach-ability

Teach-ability can be described as our ability to learn. Some people are more teachable than others. Some of us think we know all the answers. We may be rigid, inflexible, and limited by the boundaries of our fears—we put up walls. Teach-ability, however, can be learned. How teachable are you? When you're wrong, do you refuse to admit it? Do you frequently argue with others or refute ideas in your head? When you're involved in problems that aren't your fault, do you seek to explain your role? Many times, resistance to teach-ability goes along with the inability to let things go.

Your answers may reveal how your antagonistic character can impede growth. To become teachable, you must admit you don't know everything. Then you become vulnerable—a condition many people find uncomfortable. The opposite of antagonistic—highly agreeable on the outside and secretly seething—also impedes growth and change. But the rewards of teach-ability are great. We begin to learn how to exchange anger and rigidity, silence and resentment, for serenity and flexibility. We begin to grow more creative, comfortable, and secure in our new lifestyle. We become more powerful!

Be King or Queen for a Day

We can indulge ourselves occasionally, but in a different way. Instead of fantasizing about grandiose schemes and perfectionistic plans to get even or plot *Horrible Bosses*-style revenge, we can feel like kings or queens in different ways. We can take time to enjoy a walk at lunch, a movie after work, or a quick yoga session in the afternoon. It's healthy to try to escape what's uncomfortable. But change is by definition uncomfortable. A bit of fresh air and a change of scene can help us return to responsibilities with renewed energy.

Pick Your Battles

If we find ourselves often quarreling with people and feeling defiant, remember that's how frustrated children behave. We should stand our ground on what we know is right but do so calmly. And we should be ready to admit that we could be wrong. It's easier on our systems to give in occasionally. If we yield, we'll frequently find that others will too. The result may be gaining relief from tension and feeling that we've achieved a practical solution. We'll have exchanged immature behavior for relief from stress.

Take One Thing at a Time

When we're ready to give up unproductive battles, we think in grandiose terms. We are ready to surrender everything. We'll quit smoking, lose weight, begin exercising, find a relationship, return to school, and get a better job. But this isn't how we gain. This isn't proper surrender. To attempt to give up all your bad habits at once is setting yourself up for failure. Are you trying to do too much at once? Defeat your bad habits one step at a time, battle by battle.

Maintain an Escape Route

Distracting yourself is important for a successful surrender, and it's also a good practice for life in general. Spend time helping someone; volunteer in a community center or local school. Think of this as a surrender and exchange. Don't be embarrassed to say, "I'm doing this for selfish reasons." By helping others, we can learn how to surrender our will, desire, and impulses.

Keep Your Cool

The world is not a race. Practice driving within the speed limit and letting cars pass you on the freeway. Don't aggressively compete in your exercise program. When you're tempted to make a quick response, take a deep breath and let the other person complete his or her thought. Instead of watching the television, listen to soothing music. Take a leisurely bath instead of a quick shower. Exchange the frantic pace of "hi" and "bye" conversations for higher quality time with other people. Relax your sense of perfectionism—you can't smell the flowers if you never stop watering them.

Recruit an Expert

Our attempts to change old habits and attitudes may produce conflict and stress. The interacting forces both inside and around us tend to have a cumulative effect on our mental health, making little things seem worse. It may be useful to seek the help of a guidance service, a therapist, or other mental health professional. Ask a coworker or friend for a recommendation. EAPs usually provide prepaid sessions for employees and family members. Ask your human resource or personnel director if your company offers this benefit.

Write

Putting pen to paper forces us to stop and think. We sort out words, feelings, and impressions. We may be able to understand an otherwise hopelessly confusing situation only after we've taken the time to put our impressions on paper. When we read it we may notice things we hadn't seen before. Self-honesty is the cornerstone of this writing. We can fill hundreds of notebooks with meanderings on our daily life and get no closer to the peace and serenity we crave if we lack honesty. This exercise can help us see areas of our lives we're reluctant to release.

Join the Comedy Club

Stress can come from changing, coping, and the normal course of any workday. But a healthy dose of laughter helps. It can also stop you from thinking too hard. Release your sense of humor once in a while, and even learn to laugh at yourself. Humor shows us that being in control is not always synonymous to being happy.

Recognize the Levels of Power

To most of us power has a limited definition: the ability to do anything we want. But that view of power is not only immature, it feeds inflated ego. There's a higher form of power. It's achieved by recognizing and meeting needs beyond our own. By meeting other people's needs, we move a step higher on the power scale by becoming a greater asset. Through surrender and exchange, we don't lose our ability to exercise power. We give up the self-centered preoccupation with our needs only to discover that many of our needs can be met by reaching out to others.

Access Your Spiritual Side

Most religious and spiritual systems make use of surrender. Some of us have long since given up on the concept of formal religion, but we may retain abiding faith in the ways of nature or the power of logic. Still others recognize the power of a twelve-step program and the fellowship of a group that shares a Higher Power. We need to be tolerant and accepting of spiritual principles. The point is to find something that works for us. We can talk and write, but there comes a time when action must be taken. Spiritual support in any form can be an effective tool for coping with stress.

Joel describes his experience. When caught in a merger buyout, his position as a field representative for a medical services company changed literally overnight. "I knew I had to 'give in,'" he said. "I had lost my faith in this corporation and the workplace in general. I realized I had made my work my religion. Then I sat down with a friend, and he asked me to try to think of something in whose power and constancy I could truly believe. He said not to worry about whether that something could remove all my anxieties and shortcomings, just to think of something I could believe would always be there.

"Well, I'm a surfer, so the first thing that popped into my mind was the beautiful ocean. I always felt closer to the true nature of things when I was in the water, like I was a real part of the cycle. That was the closest thing I knew of then to a spiritual experience. My friend suggested that the next time I went in the water I let it flow over me and carry away those unwanted anxieties and fears. He said it sounded like I'd already been doing it without knowing. But, to me, the conscious awareness made the difference. I always left the beach freer and more joyous than before."

Joel found, after searching and experimentation, a support that he could relate to spiritually and emotionally. A belief system may help us discover faith within ourselves as we surrender those things that keep our lives frustrating and stressful. One way to increase our conscious contact with spiritual support is through prayer and meditation. These are invaluable tools in the surrender process.

Use a "Boss Box"

Try making a Boss Box. Joel tried this, too. "I found a little tin box I had saved from childhood and put in it a list of things that were bugging me. The act of writing down those things was powerful in itself, but actually putting them in my tin box and closing the lid was the most freeing thing I'd ever done. I knew then that they were out of my hands. I found that with the box I had more patience to wait things out and just do my job. I use the Boss Box quite often still and sometimes, to my surprise, I even forget what I've put in there. I know that the sooner I'm willing to surrender my concerns, the sooner they will be lifted from me. I no longer have to share my life with my obsessions."

Surrender, we find, is no longer the demon of failure we once thought it to be. It ceases to be a struggle between the good guys and the bad guys. All we need to do is admit our shortcomings, be open-minded about alternatives to our own behavior and perspective, and then be willing to surrender old ideas to gain greater rewards.

> *"Do not seek so much to be consoled, as to* console;
> *do not seek so much to be understood, as to* understand;
> *do not seek so much to be loved, as to* love. *"*
> St. Francis of Assisi

Take It Back

Recognize

1. Recognize examples of blaming, sabotage, and struggle in your job.
2. When evaluating injustices and grievances, ask yourself, Have I ever done something like this? Try and remember a specific incident. Now ask yourself, *did someone help me or overlook my mistake?* If the answer is yes, perhaps you can pass that along instead of anger and resentment.

Respond

1. Respond by brainstorming some exchanges for each situation.
2. Read the want ads. This may give you a better perspective on making the job you have more satisfying.

Reinforce

1. Before you say anything to anyone, ask yourself three things: 1) *Is it true?* 2) *Is it kind?* 3) *Is it necessary?* Use this for self-talk. It will eliminate such self-defeating statements as, "I'm stupid."
2. Practice these statements:
   - I choose balance. My life is complete with more than work.
   - I have the right to say no. I choose for myself.
   - I have a history of success. I have many talents and skills. I am not my job.

SIX

THE TIES THAT STRANGLE

"If your ship doesn't come in, swim out to meet it"
Jonathan Winters
Screenplay Writer

"We need to believe in ourselves but not to believe
that life is easy."
Jon Gardner
Author, *Self-Renewal*

Most of us learn our communication skills in the family. All too often family communication is characterized by eccentricity and, sometimes, dysfunction. Because the workplace is structured a lot like a family, individuals often fall into roles created for them in their childhood. In other words, at work we act like children. When an employee experiences discomfort and dissatisfaction with a job, he often focuses in a myopic way on his own unhappiness without looking at the larger picture of the group dynamics.

When does corporate structure become family structure? Any group of people is likely to take on the qualities of a family. But all too often in the workplace, groups can model dysfunctional families. That is, the people who make up the group, the team, or the corporation act and react in ways learned in the families in which they grew up. If that family was healthy, the child had a chance to learn from appropriate models of communication and interaction. If the family was dysfunctional, the child, now adult, will face many more challenges than the adult who learned from a more functional model.

Ann Wilson Schaef, in *The Addictive Organization*, describes the ever-increasing dysfunction of the corporate world: "We have begun to realize that many of the behaviors considered 'normal' for individuals in organizations are actually a repertoire of an active addict or a recovering codependent."

A dysfunctional family functions by controlling individual freedom. A dysfunctional system operates in the same manner, presenting limited options for employee roles or behaviors, and even limiting the way a person should think. In each dysfunctional family, it is important that certain roles are played or the system will be disrupted. The same is true in a corporation. Those around you keep you in your role in order to maintain the status quo.

ROLE-PLAYING

What are those roles? Well, in a corporation, the boss, whether the head of the team, the head of the department, or the head of the corporation, is viewed as the Father. Because of the continued male dominance in America's corporate structure, the father figure heads the hierarchy of the dysfunctional family. An employee's experience in his or her own family of origin, a loving father or an abusive one, a tyrant or a benevolent dictator, sets a model for this interaction. When the boss is viewed as the father of the family, this leaves narrowly defined and limited roles for the rest of the family—that is, the other employees.

The next most influential role in the group or family is that of the Mother. This person is responsible for caretaking, placating, or perhaps even passively dominating. In many families the mother is in fact the head of the system. Once the partner-dictatorship is established, whether abusive or benevolent, Father and Mother set the tone for the family. Perhaps the Mother is played by a management team, senior VP, or team leader. The role is to placate or mediate between disruptive forces. The Mother often says to employees, "Don't let the boss find out about that. Let's keep this between us. If you do that the CEO will be unhappy." In the dysfunctional system the mother alternately uses the image of the father figure to stress, punish, and reward the employee.

The rest can fall into stereotypic roles: the Hero, the Mascot, the Scapegoat, and the Lost Child. Let's examine each of these roles and see how they fit in the corporate structure. As you read, you may find it helpful to make notes on the relevance of the roles to your organization, personalizing each role.

The Hero

The Hero is usually the oldest child in the family, who early on assumes burdens that are inappropriate to the child's age and to what should be expected of an older sibling. With the employee in a dysfunctional system, the dynamics are the same. The Hero is the employee who assumes burdens above and beyond the job description. This employee is the "responsible one" and may be a workaholic. He or she is frequently exhausted, always under stress, and is rigid, aggressive, constantly on the go, and often self-righteous. The Hero is frequently quite charming and uses his or her charisma to advantage. Frequently, such behavior masks procrastination, insecurity, neediness, inability to set limits or delegate, and a need for acceptance for "being" rather than "doing." Because the Hero in a family is still a child, he or she competes for the parents' attention and approval. As other children enter the system, the conflict intensifies.

The Hero in the workplace can be a very disruptive influence, often setting a frenetic pace for others, failing to share responsibilities or credit, yet all the while feeling alone. "I'm the only one who can do something right. I do things the way the boss (Father/Mother) wants it to be done." This is the employee who can make others feel guilty and resentful because of the long hours and effort they appear to give to the job. Finally, this person wants and needs the attention and approval of the authority figures. In the workplace this employee needs to be recognized for being more productive than the other employees. Behind the Hero's back, coworkers may secretly resent, pity, or generally fail to respect him for his work style and work ethic. This workaholic employee is never finished and never feels satisfied. This role can have a devastating effect on anyone who assumes it.

There is often a lot of overlap between corporate roles. Even the head of a company can be left feeling like The Hero. "I felt as if I had to do everything myself because, after all, I couldn't trust others to do anything as well as I could. If you want something done right, do it yourself," Elena, a thirty-six-year-old owner and operator of a small but lucrative insurance brokerage, explains. Although she had been plagued by constant headaches, back problems, and had been warned by her physician to slow down and relax more, Elena felt that she couldn't. When she took time off from work, her employees made costly mistakes. Elena complained that her sales people made unrealistic promises to clients, promises that could have had heavy legal ramifications and errors on contracts that would be costly to the company. In her absence she complained that her employees also ran up expensive phone bills and misplaced important messages. Elena's feelings of frustration and helplessness were real. "After all the training sessions I've done with them, why did they keep making the same mistakes over and over again? I thought having a staff would ease my workload, but I spent most of my time cleaning up their messes!" Elena vacillated between treating her people with hostility and patience. In one meeting she would rant and rave about their incompetence, and in the next she would give them a pat on the back and a pep talk about how good things were going to be.

Elena had set up unrealistic expectations for herself and then had projected them onto her staff. As long as we make such unrealistic demands of ourselves, we will continue to fall short. And if we don't live up to our own expectations, we will keep blaming other people. Elena was obviously demanding perfection from her employees, a perfection that she sought at a tremendous price to herself and ultimately to her own business.

Elena felt trapped. Just two months earlier she had signed a five-year lease for her new, expanded office. What had seemed like a good idea and a wonderful dream was quickly turning into a nightmare. Although she was not aware of them, Elena had options. In any problem situation our emotional investment distorts our vision. Perhaps you can see options for Elena. She could turn over the management of her company to someone else, hire an office manager, fire her salespeople and hire more competent ones, retrain her existing staff, or sell her business. Until Elena looked at her motives and expectations of herself, she wouldn't be able to see how she had set herself up to fail. *Owning a business and managing a staff feed my ego, but is it worth my physical and mental well-being? Should my business take priority over my family? Do I really want the responsibility anymore?* Once she had taken the time to ask and answer these questions, decisions and action steps became clearer.

Elena called a meeting with her staff and announced, "I've come to a decision. I find a large organization too taxing on my health, so I've decided to work on my own." Not long after reorganizing, another broker walked into her quiet office. His first thought was that the bottom had dropped out of her business. He asked, "Where's everybody? Did they all walk out on you? Are you going out of business?"

"No," Elena replied, "I let them all go. My business is better than ever." What looked like a failure from outward appearances was really a true success story.

The initial change began when Elena stopped feeling she had no control over the circumstances. The biggest change occurred when she stopped blaming others and began to examine her own priorities. Both took less than twenty minutes. Soon, Elena's physical problems subsided. She now has more time and energy for her family, and her business runs profitably with less effort.

The Mascot

Another role is that of the Mascot (or Clown or Rebel-Without-a-Clue). This employee entertains and distracts the dysfunctional family from conflict. When stress gets too high, the Mascot is there to relieve the pressure. This person "tap dances," cracks jokes, and misbehaves in order to get the attention of the authority figures and take the focus off of the real problems.

In a dysfunctional family the father may be drunk and the mother may threaten to leave. This Mascot child then gets into trouble at school, creating drama and leading the focus away from the mother's threats and the father's alcoholism. In an organization, it is very much the same. When the stakes are high—it looks like a merger might be pending and layoffs coming—this employee distracts other employees from constructive activity by refusing to take things seriously, by suggesting misbehavior, or by creating rumors that feed distraction rather than problem-solving or fact-finding.

Very often the Mascot is well liked, popular, and witty. The person may be viewed as eccentric. "That's just the way Ted is. You know Ted; he's always making a joke!" This can be the "bad boy" (or girl) in a company. He or she is the rebel who is benevolently viewed by other employees, given a pat on the head, and perhaps not taken seriously. This employee is probably unhappy and not very productive. Such an employee's sense of self-esteem is negatively affected by this kind of behavior.

The Scapegoat

The Scapegoat can be a person or group of people on whom we blame a problem. "Well, if personnel would just get its act together . . ." "If marketing weren't so demanding . . ." "If corporate didn't make such arbitrary decisions . . ." The Scapegoat allows us to give up our responsibility for solving the problems. We now have an excuse for not trying to change situations. We blame and hope that the problems will go away. In the family, this is the child who gets sick when the parents are drinking too much. This is the child who often gets caught when siblings quarrel and misbehave, or becomes the suspected culprit when mischief is discovered. All fingers automatically point to the Scapegoat.

The Scapegoat is a role that many people are taught to play and continue to play as adults. This person may resemble the Mascot—entertaining and rebellious, but always taking the focus off of us and the real problems. The dynamics of blaming are necessary for dysfunctional systems to maintain homeostasis—the status quo.

"I worked for a large telemarketing firm," relates Salina, who experienced firsthand the enmeshment of these roles. "We actually referred to our supervisor as 'Big Daddy' even though she was a woman. I don't know where the name 'Big Daddy' came from. I just know all the employees called her that. Big Daddy was erratic in her praise as well as her criticism of us. Sometimes I would reach very high totals of sales and closings, yet she would criticize me for not doing more. On other days when I looked a little blue or came in a couple of minutes late, she might be very sympathetic. I know that she made me feel like a child. That was bad enough, but the employee who got all of our sympathy was Joanna. She couldn't do anything right and got nothing but blame. I wondered why she stayed. She was accused of the most outrageous things. I think her mistreatment of Joanna hurt me more than her mistreatment of me."

Salina describes very graphically the process of dysfunction in the workplace. A competent woman, a good worker, she fell into the pattern of childlike discomfort, even fear, around "Big Daddy," the person who was unpredictable in both praise and discipline. Like a child, Salina began to second-guess and attempt to mind-read, trying very hard to please and forgetting work goals. She eventually left the company. "I needed to be in a situation where I was rewarded more consistently. I was making good money in that company and my commissions were high.

But the stress of trying to anticipate the moods of my supervisor and the unpredictability of the system just took too much of a toll. And I just couldn't stand seeing anyone abused like Joanna was."

The Lost Child

Another role played in the family is that of the Unseen, or Lost Child. This is a good child who does what is expected, does not create problems, but all too often is overlooked when rewards and attention are doled out. This employee is a team player, but doesn't have the flair, the drama, or the problems to draw the attention of the boss. This employee may feel overlooked and unappreciated. This worker frequently picks up the pieces for other employees then feels resentful because no credit or attention is paid to his or her efforts on behalf of the team.

The lost child, or the lost employee, is a valuable worker, yet is prey to other job offers or quietly seeks a new position. If you are such a person, you do not have to change your job; rather, change your behavior in order to get the appreciation you deserve. If this is a coworker, you may be helpful in assisting that person to become more vocal in order for the team to function more productively. This person would make an excellent partner.

Happily Ever After

In this chapter we see that groups of people in companies, as in society and families, tend to be more alike than they are different. They accept or take on roles that may not be comfortable, but are at least familiar. Sometimes the behavior of one person dictates the roles available to other members of the group. When the employee becomes the Dad, the Mom, or the Mascot, the other employees escape roles that require confrontation or effort. A person who might do well as a supervisor may back down or take a more subservient role rather than try to challenge a Hero, who has already assumed that personality.

The corporation is not a family. These roles need not be real. Reality is job descriptions and work behaviors. Your next step is to separate dysfunctional and remembered roles from actual job descriptions, personalities, and necessary functions in the workplace. In looking at these dysfunctional roles we see that there are specific dynamics that allow the roles to continue to be played.

These roles and the dynamics that keep them in place are not easy to understand. If this is your first introduction to the concepts, you may wish to do some additional reading or participate in self-help groups and twelve-step programs like Codependent Anonymous and Adult Children of Alcoholics. If you're ready to move on, the first step in dealing with codependency in a company is to identify the roles that people on your team may be playing. Relate those dynamics to your own role. Then it's time to consider a change or take a risk by changing your own behavior and stepping out of the assigned role.

MIND YOUR MIND

Enabling is a term describing behavior, conscious and unconscious, that allows or encourages addiction. It is a dynamic that maintains dysfunctional behavior. For example, a husband may wish that his wife stop drinking. When she turns down wine at dinner, which he enjoys in moderation, he may say, "Oh, come on, just have one glass." In this way he falsely pretends that his wife can limit her drinking to one glass of wine, denying her alcoholism and giving her a mixed message. On one hand he wants her to quit drinking, but on the other hand he says it is okay to drink. He stays in control; she is off-balance as he enables her to drink.

In an organization, people enable by using silence, by failing to confront, by going along with the group, by acceding to peer pressure. For example, a secretary is asked by his boss if he would mind working late tonight. Instead of saying, "Yes, I would mind, I have already made plans with my family," "No, I wouldn't mind just this once, but I will make up the time with a long lunch tomorrow," or clarifying that his additional hours would be recompensed as overtime pay, the secretary responds by saying, "Well . . ."

Then the boss says, "It's up to you."

And the secretary, feeling pressured, says, "It's okay, I guess . . ."

This is an example of enabling behavior. The secretary enabled the boss to get what he wanted by not speaking up or asking for time to think. Both engaged in dysfunctional behavior, creating resentment and anger on the part of the employee. The employee not only failed to be recompensed for the additional work and enabled the boss to expect him to give in next time, but will also probably get even in ways that harm the entire company.

DESPERATE COWORKERS

Reality television is another dynamic that thrives on dysfunction. "Reality" stars unnecessarily dramatize regular office operations and other communication. It's not restricted to daytime television. Drama in an organization is ongoing, unrelenting, and usually has to do with gossip, distraction, and overreaction.

Janet describes an experience in the data entry department where seventeen men and women enter data from insurance forms. Some might see the work as boring, but it is a critically important function in the organization. Often this group distracts itself with gossip and chitchat, though they still maintain a high level of productivity due to their experience.

Janet had just walked in and heard everyone conversing loudly. She asked what the buzz was about.

"Mandatory carpooling!" was the answer. "They are going to make us all carpool. They've got a consultant coming in. They're laying out grids, and we are going to be told who lives in our neighborhood. Then we are going to be given thirty days to start carpooling with those people."

Janet laughed. "Where did such a rumor get started?"

"Well, it's very serious!" they all chimed in.

Janet knew that mandatory carpooling was a ludicrous idea and wouldn't happen. Surely it violated several civil rights and would have been a first for any company. However, the group was so invested in the drama and so distracted from their work they failed to recognize any rational input.

That's Classified

The secret is another workplace dynamic that maintains the status quo of addiction and is a dominant force in dysfunctional families. Consider a situation where there's a proverbial "elephant in the living room," an issue so obstructing that it's ignored. A family is sitting around watching television; one member of the family—a father, a daughter, a relative—is visibly drunk. A visitor comes to the door, enters, and immediately notices the elephant in the room. No one mentions it, and the visitor is invited to sit down and watch television with the group. All of them conscientiously ignore the issue, and will even when the visitor is gone.

Ramon is a newly elected vice president in a large software development corporation. Upon a promotion to vice president he was given access to a company car. He was happily surprised to discover this was one of the perks of his job. At the same time this company was engaged in severe cost-cutting. Expenses of all sorts were under close scrutiny. Ramon wondered why the company continued to provide a seemingly nonessential benefit. The firm was relatively small and did not attract the types of executives who required such perks. One of Ramon's first high-level corporate meetings involved a budget review of the administrative aspects of the program. Ramon knew that expenses such as travel and corporate cars would be part of this review, and he expected to lose his company car.

Each member of the C-suite had been provided a copy of the budget for review. Ramon had conscientiously reviewed his and made many notations that he might bring up in the meeting. As the meeting proceeded, Ramon became aware of an undercurrent in the room. He realized that this budget was not going to be seriously attacked. He found himself pulling back when items he had marked for discussion were brought to the table. He waited for the company cars to be considered. The item was passed over by the CFO chairing the meeting. Ramon did not speak up. He left the meeting wondering about the hypocrisy of this group. They were requiring severe cutbacks on supplies and operating expenses for the departments, and yet they were unwilling to recognize some fat in their own budget. At the same time, as a new vice president, he was reluctant to mention this fact to anyone. Doing so would have proved risky, and so his realization became his secret.

A secret is not necessarily something dramatic, exciting, or an item that will tear down the foundations of a corporation with scandal and notoriety. A secret is simply something we observe, are bothered by, and fail to address. Like secrets in families, secrets in organizations are usually very destructive.

The Ties that Strangle

In understanding dysfunctional systems, the term "codependence" represents an important component. Codependence may be defined as a constellation of behaviors that emerge from exposure to addictive systems.

The codependent is characterized by a behavioral style in which emotional wellness is dictated by the actions and reactions of other people. In other words, the codependent looks to others to make him or her feel good. At the same time a perceived slight or careless word from another can cause feelings of rejection or injury.

The codependent in the workplace is a passive-aggressive communicator specializing in highly indirect communication. This results in mixed messages and confused communication. Often the codependent will agree on the surface, express the passive aggressive component through some subtle sabotage such as missing deadlines, overly perfectionistic work, demands, etc. Frequently others are blamed for resultant delays and mistakes.

Here are some other traits associated with codependence.

Making Nice:	Hides hidden or denied hostility; covers repressed emotions.
Serving Others:	Provides a facade of helpfulness often accompanied by a long-suffering attitude; martyrdom; "It's all on my shoulders" statements.
Caretaking:	Often takes the form of a domination and manipulation. A substance-abusing partner is often associated with codependent caretakers.
Good Listening:	May disguise a need to control and manipulate others through rumor, manipulation, and indirect communication.
Victimization:	Related to the picture of an overburdened martyr, the codependent often portrays self as a victim, or is central to many dramas, usually self-created.

Depression: Is often associated with codependence as
                 the individual's control and manipulation
                 tactics fail to produce the desired feelings,
                 e.g., love, affection, loyalty.

Negativity: Being a "wet blanket;" opposing change
                 and generally expressing insecurity and
                 rigidity of thinking when creativity or
                 movement is called for in the workplace.

Notice that any one of these traits taken alone may be normal, ordinary, and even positive, such as good listening. Codependent people exhibit several of these characteristics in the extreme. Individuals emerging from alcoholic families are likely to exhibit codependence to some degree. When the dynamics of the dysfunctional family are recreated in the workplace, it is easy for an adult child of addictive parents to fall into old behaviors. Addiction, whether in the form of workaholism or substance abuse, occurs only with the support of codependence.

Can We Talk?

There are many negative aspects in bringing the model of family into the workplace. I have described the dysfunctional family—although we all know what that looks like! But can the family model serve as a positive example for dynamics in the workplace? Absolutely. This can be a good way of helping employees to redefine their roles, change dynamics of their behavior, and stop the elements of dysfunction.

In a happy, healthy family, communication is direct and open. Confrontation is not feared, and emphasis is placed on changing negative behavior rather than taking sides. The same is true of an organization. When dysfunctional behavior and the enabling dynamics are removed, there is freedom for direct communication, constructive confrontation, greater creativity and productivity. Employees then are free to experience different roles, including leadership.

And the roles that we have previously described can be very useful when communication is open. At times a Mascot can distract the group to break the level of tension. Sometimes a group should blame the anonymous corporate entity, the budget, or the economy in order to take the focus off their powerlessness. It is frequently useful to have someone protect us or go to bat for us or support us if we are in a confrontation, like healthy parents and office Heroes might do.

The problem exists not in the words or roles of mother, father, child, but only when roles are established to limit choices. If we function without choices, or as though we are not responsible, mature adults, then we as employees will not be productive in situations that require creativity, communication, and problem solving. The loyalties of a family, the love and interdependence, can serve as positive examples of how a company can function. These are qualities of empowerment.

TAKE IT BACK

Recognize

1. Identify the role you play in your organization (you may play more than one role).
2. Identify the aspects of this role that are positive and the aspects that are negative.
3. Would you like to change this role?
4. What role, or combination of roles, would you prefer to play in your organization?
5. What hinders you from playing this role? Pay special attention to enabling, secrets, codependency, and drama.

Respond

1. Having identified the roles and the dynamics keeping this role in place, respond with your feelings about each aspect of these roles and dynamics. For example, "When I recognize that I am enabling my boss to give me vague directions, I feel like a kid. I'm angry at myself and embarrassed." Or, "I see that I am most like the Hero. I feel best when I know someone else needs me. I don't like having to do so much work to feel good about myself."

2. Make two columns on a sheet of blank paper, and on one side list the role or dynamic (e.g., secrets, enabling) and in the other column the feelings that that role elicits in you (e.g., anger, fear).

Reinforce

1. Commit to explore the roles in your own family of origin. Perhaps attending a twelve-step self-help group such as Adult Children of Alcoholics or Codependents Anonymous can be a first step.
2. Check local bookstores in the self-help section for information on dysfunctional families and alcoholism.
3. Repeat this statement: "Time has healed the wounds of the past. I am free to be me."

SEVEN

COPING WITH ANGER

*"Peace is not something you wish for. It is something
you make, something you do, something you are, and
something you give away."*
Robert Fulghum

*"The only way you can achieve true revenge is not
to let your enemies cause you to self-destruct."*
Harvey Mackay

Anger is one of the most destructive forces in the workplace today. It is ultimately a fatal emotion. Studies show that about 20 percent of us have hostility levels high enough to be dangerous—to our own health and to those around us. A high hostility level is associated with increased smoking, drinking, eating, and weight gain. Hostility has long been a contributor to coronary risk and heart disease, as well as myriad other illnesses.

It's likely you have experienced the relationship between anger, depression, resentment, and low self-esteem. You know about the aches and pains that come from tension, the fatigue and lack of joy that ensue as days get increasingly filled with the burden of suppressed rage. Paul describes the hostile atmosphere he endured for over three years in his position as quality engineer in a large fabrication department of a microchip company.

THE BOILING POINT

"The head of the company had a philosophy that people worked best under stress," Paul remembers. "The senior managers emulated him by putting impossible deadlines on projects, arbitrarily rejecting products, and trashing work that was already passed for shipment. At first I didn't understand, and then one of the team leaders under my supervision clued me in. I became very angry. I tried to talk to my department head about the destructive nature of this practice. I even naively quoted studies showing how reward motivates employees and negativity reduces productivity. Once more I got 'clued in.' 'This is how the president works,' I was told.

"Now I was not only angry, but felt powerless. I was trapped. I had just relocated my wife and two kids—one just starting a new middle school—and my wife had found a job she really loved in the new area. And the benefits were good. Plus I began to feel I needed to protect the fabrication workers. By staying I could absorb some of the craziness and let them keep working. Boy, was I wrong!

"Headaches, nightmares, a rash on both arms, and general irritability were only a few of the symptoms that came with this deal. I went to my doctor about the rash, and we started to talk.

"The whole story came out. He said I should quit. I just laughed. I found myself avoiding meetings so I wouldn't blurt something out. I missed some important design changes that ultimately impacted the workers I was trying to protect. I took more sick days and just sat at home watching television. I was drinking, and I don't even like the stuff. I was growing angrier and angrier."

Paul got lucky. This privately-held company was purchased by a larger corporation, and then everything changed. With the new management, a different philosophy—one that Paul subscribed to—came into being. His methods were now valued. But Paul didn't just relax. He decided to get some help for the lingering resentment and anger he felt. Paul saw an ad for an anger management course and enrolled. With anger management, people can take the positive aspects of an emotion (like energy and adrenaline) and turn them to positive use. At the same time, anger management includes controlling or eliminating the negative aspects (self-denigration, acting out, harming others). Note that this definition does not mean you never get angry. Accepting life on life's terms is a part of any plan for improved communication. The emotion of anger has a positive and protective value to humans.

To begin a program of anger management, let's define a few terms. Confrontation is a word that most people react to in a negative manner. "I hate confrontation," is a common response. A slightly different view defines constructive confrontation as a technique of bringing feelings and facts to bear on a situation, with a plan in mind for positive resolution. Thus, confrontation takes on a positive and less aggressive tone. Constructive confrontation includes elements of self-assessment, rehearsal, objectivity, and sometimes coaching.

ANGER BIG AND SMALL

Jackson teaches in a community college and shares a desk with a coworker in a cubbyhole of an office. Jackson comes in on alternate days to his peer, so the arrangement should've worked out. But each time Jackson arrived, he found the desk cluttered with crumpled paper, dirty coffee cups, and food scraps. At first Jackson cleaned the desk, thinking his coworker might get the message. When the trash continued to appear, Jackson left it stacked in a pile with his colleague's name on it. Nothing helped.

Jackson complained to his wife over and over. When she suggested he confront his coworker, he replied, "It's just so petty. I don't want to make an issue of it." Yet, just as Jackson made the statement to his wife, he realized what an issue it had become for him. Recalling a recent training he had attended on negotiation and confrontation, he decided to try for a positive approach and deal directly with his peer.

The technique of constructive confrontation emphasizes the positive elements of direct and honest communication. In this example Jackson had become increasingly preoccupied with the problem and was taking it home; he realized that his indirect ways of dealing with the situation would not work to relieve his discomfort.

Jackson took action. He came to the shared office when he knew his coworker would be available. Simply and directly he stated his request for a cleaner workspace. His desk mate seemed a little embarrassed and agreed to dispose of the trash and clean the desk after he left each day. Jackson thanked him and left. What had become a nagging obsession was dead within the space of minutes, and Jackson felt tremendous relief.

ANGER KILLS

Mario's anger caused emotional pain as he endured a hostile and demeaning situation at work, but he also began to have physical pain. His story begins with his boss's anger and frustration, the trickle-down effect falling hardest upon Mario.

Mario is a clerical support and works for a large aerospace company that recently went through extensive reorganization. Mario is well-liked, bright, and has a positive attitude about the future. However, when he talks about problems on the job it's in whispered tones, and a muscle in his cheek seems to twitch. His discomfort is obvious. "My new boss would come back from a corporate meeting and bark orders: 'Do this! Why hasn't this been done? You are the sloppiest jerk I've ever worked with!' You know the kind of abuse. His rage spared no one.

"I'm a good worker. I've always been given great reviews, and I like the work. Some people think it's boring, but I'm an organized kind of guy. After one of these screaming sessions was over and this boss had stormed into his office and slammed the door, I'd feel like I was possessed. My head would pound, I'd get stabbing pains in my chest and my stomach would flip-flop. Weeks of this went by. Then something weird happened. I began stuffing small supplies into my backpack that I carry to and from work. I began with inexpensive items first—pens, paper clips, and stuff like that. Then I took more and more valuable items; my small, petty revenge got bigger."

Not only was Mario hurt, angry, and physically debilitated, he was compounding the problem by acting in contradiction to his own values. His actions had begun to make him feel like a liar and a thief. He felt guilty about the items he had taken, but didn't feel any better when he had returned some of them. Mario decided he would have to confront the boss or quit. Neither alternative seemed practical. He sought the help of a specialist. The process was not a long one. Together he and the specialist developed a strategy for a constructive confrontation. But first Mario needed to learn the six checkpoints for dealing with anger.

Six Checkpoints

Not all situations involving anger can be dealt with through communication. Obviously, when anger involves violence and rage, other alternatives must be used. However, for most situations in daily living, constructive confrontation can be very effective, *if* these six conditions can be met:

1. Expressions of feelings should be directed at the target of the anger.

2. The expression is meant to restore your sense of control and sense of justice.

3. The expression provides opportunity for the other person to change.

4. The expression must change the behavior of the target or give you new insights.

5. You and your target must speak the same language.

6. Seek agreement from the other person that there will be no retaliation.

Let's review the parameters of each of these conditions.

1. *Expressions of feelings must be directed at the target of the anger.* Mario was expressing his anger at the company, his coworkers, and himself—not at the boss. In counseling he agreed to confront the supervisor directly but did not know how.

2. *The expression is meant to restore your sense of control and sense of justice.* Mario momentarily satisfied his anger in stealing, but in the long run it added to his feeling of powerlessness. He was creating more injustice and compounding his feeling of losing control by acting in a way that he found reprehensible. His next step was to be directed outside himself.

3. *The expression provides opportunity for the other person to change.* Mario balked at this one. "I don't want to hurt him," he said, "I just want him to stop." The clinician helped Mario see that a sense of getting even was necessary in order to feel better. This did not necessarily involve any real action and certainly no intended hurt toward another. In any situation of hurt, we often desire to hurt others only to ensure that they will know how we feel. "I just wanted him to know what it felt like," was an expression Mario had previously used when referring to the humiliation of being screamed at and called names. The specialist asked Mario if he thought the other man knew what he looked like when he was screaming and yelling. "I doubt it," was the reply. Often simply drawing attention to the behavior may be

punishment enough for the other person. Sometimes just being forced to listen is an appropriate punishment. Maybe you can remember the childhood feelings of being "talked to." You can even feel your stomach flip when a significant other says, "We need to talk."

4. *The expression must change the behavior of the target or give you new insights.* In this situation, Mario had nothing to lose. The worst case scenario was that nothing would change. He still had the alternative of resigning. If the boss refused to listen or was unwilling to change, Mario would then have the understanding that reason and communication would not work with his boss. He could take pride in knowing that he had tried and regained control of what he could change.

5. *You and your target must speak the same language.* In developing prepared notes for the meeting, Mario was encouraged to use actual words that the boss had used. Also, Mario's boss was generally a rational person and a good communicator—both traits Mario would try and mirror. Again, these conditions do not apply when situations have become abusive.

6. *Seek agreement from the other person that there will be no retaliation.* Mario knew that his boss might become angry. Now Mario began to fear that he could be fired. The clinician suggested that Mario discuss the planned confrontation with the human resources coordinator. Mario wanted to know what his rights were in this situation. He was advised to begin by getting an agreement from his boss that he would listen without interrupting until Mario had finished. Mario was also assured that he could not be fired. The company guidelines for termination were reviewed.

Mario prepared well for his confrontation. He rehearsed with a coworker who had a quick temper and a style much like Mario's boss. In one scenario that they rehearsed, the boss exploded and threatened to fire Mario. They practiced Mario's control and response. In the other scenario the boss was more reasonable.

The actual situation was tense. Mario began by asking for the boss's agreement to listen. He received a snide, "Don't I always?" Mario began to stammer but continued by expressing a positive statement about having learned a lot since the two of them had begun to work together. This was certainly a true statement. The boss seemed flattered and relaxed a little. Mario then began to talk about specific situations. "I notice that when you attend the director's meetings, you often return angry and upset. You then berate me, raising your voice, calling me names, and swearing." Mario went on, being very specific and using the actual words the boss had used.

As the boss listened, Mario reported that he could see the embarrassment and humiliation in his face. Like many bullies, this individual pretended that everyone just forgot the behavior and went on as though nothing had happened. When caught, he was indeed ashamed. He expressed his feelings to Mario, who listened with relief and surprise. This was the "retaliation-revenge" that helped Mario to feel some sense of justice. He felt validated and relieved.

Ultimately the boss agreed to change. And he did. While his basic style of quick temper and lashing out could still appear, it was clear to Mario that the boss was more aware and under control. Mario was also able to speak out more quickly to short-circuit any diatribes. They began to work together more successfully.

While each of us must practice and learn which strategies will work with our own situations and style, always try a technique before you discard it. Don't say, "Well, that worked okay for Mario, but you don't know what my boss is like. She'd fire me on the spot." Enlist the help of a friend, coworker, or family member. Review the six rules and see if the conditions can be met for planning a constructive confrontation.

THE F WORD

Ross worked for a small printing plant. He had been happily employed for more than ten years as plant supervisor. When the plant was sold to a larger firm he was pleased to learn that his position rated a substantial raise. He was also excited about some new equipment and advanced technology that was being introduced. Within the first week after the takeover he received a memo stating that no employee would be credited with more than two weeks' vacation time. Reasons were given, but Ross just saw red. He had over six weeks accumulated vacation leave, and he and his wife had planned a long road-trip in their new recreational vehicle across Canada. Ross could not get his new employer to give him the time off he felt he deserved. He was furious. As days passed and his anger and resentment preoccupied him, Ross realized he had to get over it, but he wasn't sure how.

This is an example where constructive confrontation, assertive behavior, and other techniques do not apply. Ross was harmed by a faceless entity. There was no one to confront, no action to be taken to restore any sense of justice. He decided instead to use the technique of forgiveness.

"Forgive? Isn't that a word for church or people who don't stick up for themselves? And anyway, I was wronged, and I didn't do anything!" Think of anger and resentment like the air you breathe into a balloon. No matter how little or how much you blow, the air fills the balloon completely. So it is with anger—a little or a lot, active and loud or quiet and sullen—it fills the person completely. The balloon, like Ross, ultimately bursts. His breaking point led to migraines, sleeplessness, and family disharmony.

Be Selfish

Forgiveness is selfish. In the popular *How to Forgive Your Ex-Husband*, authors Marcia Hootman and Patt Perkins state that releasing resentment is essential for well-being. They describe the process as both physical and mental. Consider this scenario: A feeling of resentment enters your mind. It becomes a part of your mind, leeching off your thoughts. Each time you are reminded of the resentment, you feel pain—like feeling a sore tooth with your tongue or being continually irritated by a small paper cut on your finger. Resentment now controls you. You must take action to regain control.

Forgiveness is an action step. It involves completing the relationship with the person or situation; releasing your attachment to the form of punishment (the blame, resentment, the betrayal) of the relationship; and *recontexting* the relationship. The context of a situation or dialogue with another person is like the background in a photograph. Have you ever taken a great picture of a child or friend only to find the background—a messy living room, an unmade bed—spoiled the shot? Changing that background is "recontexting."

For example, take the image of your boss making a sarcastic comment about your work and turn the background into any angry board meeting in which her boss is shaking a fist. Or picture an angry coworker making excuses for not meeting a deadline against a background of all the times you failed to keep an agreement. While this technique may not elicit sympathy from you, it does help you picture the situation differently. Changing your point of view, your perspective on what the other person was feeling or thinking, is also recontexting. This process can change expectations and allow communication to be more open and direct.

Focus on each technique whether it is constructive confrontation, recontexting, or forgiveness as an act of selfishness. You want things to be better for you. Ultimately improving things for yourself is like throwing a small pebble into a pond: the ripples begin small and get larger and larger, affecting the whole surface over time. By using just one of the techniques described in this chapter you are throwing that small stone, with its positive ripples to coworkers, family, friends, but most of all, enhancing your self-worth and your own productivity in the workplace.

Forgiveness is a very practical word. The action step is to stop talking about the problem. As long as we continue to talk and blame bosses and coworkers for their behaviors, real or imagined, there is no forgiveness, and thus no moving on. Failing to forgive, confront, or constructively correct has the biggest negative effect on the person who retains the anger and resentment. But he or she also has the most to gain by forgiveness. By forgiving the boss and getting on with the job, you are taking action to improve the quality of your own life. Forgiveness is especially useful when someone very close to you, perhaps unseen and unknown, has wronged you. In these cases there is little you can do that will have an impact on what was done to you. You cannot confront them or make them aware of the hurt you've felt. In any case, forgiving is a process with a beginning, a middle, and an end. And in order to work, each step must be taken carefully.

How to Forgive

1. Consciously identify how you were wronged and how it made you feel, how it affected you, your family, your future, or your emotional well-being. It is important to be specific. Relatively minor wrongs can sometimes be removed at this point. "I was angry when I spilled copy machine toner on the carpet. I forgave myself. I hurt no one, I was inconvenienced by sixty-nine seconds, and I have more toner. I'm over it." It will help to write down exactly what you think was done to you. For example, "My supervisor ruined my life. Everyone was laughing at me," may be what you think happened. Now write

down exactly what was done to you. "My supervisor contradicted me in front of the CEO. She made me seem like I wasn't prepared. I felt humiliated and embarrassed." As you write, some perspective may be obtained. Anger and resentment cannot exist without some degree of self-deception.

2. Make a policy decision, an agreement with yourself that you willingly choose to forgive the wrong—the transgression—for selfish reasons. You forgive in order to get on with your job and your life. Forgiveness is an act of grace. You are being a gracious person by forgiving.

3. Note that forgiveness does not equate with forgetting. You can maintain and probably should remember what had been done to you. You may choose not to trust that person again, or it may take some time before you can drop your guard. Understand that you can remember the act and protect yourself from being hurt in the same way or by the same person in the future: Remember, to err is human, to forgive divine, and to forget, foolhardy.

4. Now the most difficult part of this process: Stop talking about it. This may be the biggest challenge to completing the process. After interviews with literally hundreds of women, Patt Perkins observed, "The stories sounded as though they had happened yesterday. The teller became angry, often cried, was dramatic, sad, seemed to suffer the pain and feelings all over again. I wondered how many times these stories had to be told before they could be told objectively, without emotion, without the drama, or how many times they had to be told before the teller was bored by her own telling."

Anger is all too often a social occasion. It frequently disappears when it loses its audience. If the second step, forgiveness, cannot be completed, you might need additional help, perhaps professional. In practicing this step, start with small matters. Recognize when an injustice has been done to you, and use the situation for practice. Don't start with longstanding or traumatic grievances; work up to those.

Self-talk or affirmations may be useful for accomplishing many behavior changes connected to forgiveness. Try these self-talk statements.

- I have done a similar thing. I remember when I _____. Someone excused me.
- I know ____ did the best he or she could at the time. My single explanation is not explanation enough.
- I willingly release the past. It is safe for me to let go.
- I choose to heal this rift. I declare peace and go forward.
- Let's start over. I'll take the first step by ____ (e.g., admitting my part).

ABCs of Self-Talk

All anger begins with a thought—a perception that wrong has been done, that we have been hurt, that someone has caused pain. Anyone can recognize anger when it explodes. In coping with difficult situations, it is critical to recognize the starting point in the process of becoming angry or resentful. Take the next step of becoming the master of anger, not a victim.

Rhonda, new to her job in software training, describes a disturbing situation she experienced in her office. Because she works for a large national company and does training all over the nation, she must attend frequent meetings to receive changed orders, new information, and schedules. Like most meetings, these seldom started on time. Rhonda, by contrast, is always early and likes to feel prepared and settled. She became increasingly angry as latecomers straggled in and casual chitchat occupied the group leader.

What started out as a pet peeve became a hijacking force. Rhonda tried to busy herself with work to distract herself from her growing anger, but found she could not concentrate. She then tried to read a book but felt embarrassed and unprofessional. She found the anger and resentment occupying her mind after the meeting had started. Finally, at an important decision-making point, the chairperson asked Rhonda's opinion. She was mortified. She had no idea what was being discussed. This has got to stop, she told herself.

Rhonda was able to successfully use a technique called self-talk. To stop her obsessive thoughts, she went through a simple three-step procedure that I call the ABCs of self-talk.

A. When her thoughts drifted to lateness, she said to herself, "Stop! Thank you, mind, for sharing. Now shut up!" She then adjusted her thoughts with a simple prayer. (A song, childhood rhyme, or poem will do.)

B. Breathing deeply, she changed her posture, sat more erectly, and recrossed her legs.

C. Then she congratulated herself. "Good job, Rhonda." Even if the thought drifted back in, she simply began with "A" again, saying "Stop," and recited more of her "mantra."

The three-step system is:

A. Adjust your thoughts when a reaction begins. Say, silently or aloud, "STOP!" Then say to yourself, *"God grant me the serenity to accept the things I cannot change, the courage to change the things I can, and the wisdom to know the difference."*

B. Breathe deeply from the diaphragm and change your posture. Relax the shoulders, uncross legs, unclench fists, and look in a different direction.

C. Congratulate yourself. Even though the thought returns, you have begun. Remember, as my friend Tom Martin is fond of saying, "If you blow on a saxophone every day, you may not learn to be a good player, but you will learn how to blow it."

Win the Next One

Often when facilitating stress management seminars, I asked the question, "How many of you have ever read an article on stress management?" Almost every hand in the room goes up. The next question is, "How many of you have read two articles on the same subject?" Most hands stay up. "What did you learn from the second article that you hadn't read in the first one?" Laughing, one or two in the group volunteer, "Nothing." When we discuss why individuals keep reading more articles on stress management and attending this seminar, the answer is we are looking for something new, easier: a quick fix.

A while back I found an audio-tape program labeled, "The Six-Second Stress Cure." That naturally appealed to me. Wow, relaxing and ending stress in six seconds. Being rushed, and stressed, I put it into my car player while I drove to my next appointment. The author began by saying, "It takes about six months of practice to learn this technique." There are no quick fixes, and there is definitely nothing new under the sun. Research continues to validate the efficacy of prayer and spiritual exercise, the role of community service in improving the quality of life, the therapeutic aspects of pet care, being around children, and giving service to the chronically ill. You already know these techniques sound dated and trite, but they still work in coping with anger.

At this point in your reading it is probably clear that you must commit some time to improving your job situation and your state of mind. You must devote some energy and take some risks. In order to get something, it is likely you will have to give. No matter what the problem or conditions of your job, eventually you will have to make a choice. You will either have to accept the conditions or make a change. These suggestions, I hope, will inspire you not to resign yourself to martyrdom, but to make a change. You have control over the kind of life you have in the workplace.

Don't let anger, cynicism, and feelings of defeat keep you from moving on to a more positive focus. If you keep working on yourself you can experience less frustration and enjoy your job. Author Betty Harragan says, "Failure in the sports culture is not treated as a demoralizing agent, but as a revitalizing force. Losing a game is the signal to practice more, to improvise better techniques . . . to go forward with determination to win the next one."

Take It Back

Recognize

1. Make a list of situations, past and present, in which you have become very angry.
2. Differentiate these situations from the next list, things that you resent.

Respond

1. Respond to each of the situations, grudges, and peeves you have listed with a technique from this chapter, or one that you've successfully used in the past.

Reinforce

1. To reinforce your commitment to your own emotional well-being, take the test below to assess your anger style. Let the results guide you to more action steps.
2. Consider this affirmation: "I take only peace and harmony within myself and my job. I listen to the pleasant and the good. I release the pattern of behavior in me that attracted this experience. I take only good in my life."

ASSESS YOUR ANGER STYLE

This inventory offers you an opportunity to make an objective self-study of how anger affects you and how you deal with it in your daily contacts with others. It allows you to identify a style for insight as well as behavioral change.

Please answer each question on Figure 7 as quickly as you can according to the way you feel most of the time. Put a check in only one of the blanks.

figure 7		
	Yes	No
1. Do you admit that you are angry when asked?	__	__
2. Do you have a tendency to take your anger out on someone other than the person you are angry with?	__	__
3. When you are angry with someone, do you discuss it with that person?	__	__
4. Do you keep things in until you finally explode with anger?	__	__
5. Do you pout or sulk for a long time when someone hurts your feelings?	__	__
6. Do you disagree with others even though they might get angry?	__	__
7. Do you hit others when you get angry?	__	__
8. Does it upset you a great deal when someone disagrees with you?	__	__
9. Do you express your ideas when they differ from those of others?	__	__
10. Do you have a tendency to be very critical of others?	__	__
11. Are you satisfied with the way you settle your differences with others?	__	__
12. Is it very difficult for you to say nice things to other people?	__	__
13. Do you have good control of your temper?	__	__
14. Do you become depressed very easily?	__	__
15. When a problem arises between you and another person, do you discuss it without losing control of your emotions?	__	__
16. Do you have a tendency to criticize or put down other people?	__	__
17. When someone has hurt your feelings do you discuss the matter with that person?	__	__
18. Do you have frequent arguments with others?	__	__
19. Do you often feel like hitting someone else?	__	__
20. Do you sometimes feel anger toward someone you love?	__	__
21. Do you sometimes have strong urges to do something harmful?	__	__
22. Do you keep your cool when you are angry with someone?	__	__
23. Do you tend to feel very guilty after getting angry at someone?	__	__
24. When you become angry, do you pull away or withdraw from people?	__	__
25. When someone is angry with you, do you automatically or quickly strike back with your own anger?	__	__
26. Are you aware of when you are angry?	__	__
27. Provided the timing is appropriate, do you express your angry feelings without exploding?	__	__
28. Do you tend to make cutting remarks to others?	__	__
29. Do you control yourself when things do not go your way?	__	__
30. Do you feel that anger is a normal emotion?	__	__

Circle each of your "yes" answers in the boxes on Figure 8. For example, if you answered "yes" to question 1, circle it. If you answered "no" do not record a circle.

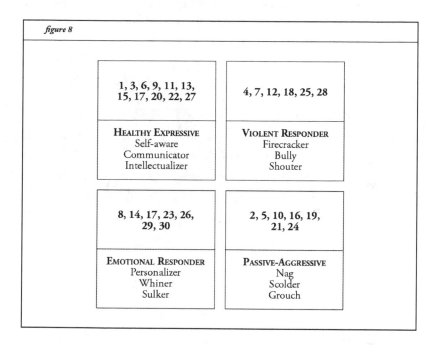

figure 8

1, 3, 6, 9, 11, 13, 15, 17, 20, 22, 27	4, 7, 12, 18, 25, 28
HEALTHY EXPRESSIVE Self-aware Communicator Intellectualizer	**VIOLENT RESPONDER** Firecracker Bully Shouter
8, 14, 17, 23, 26, 29, 30	2, 5, 10, 16, 19, 21, 24
EMOTIONAL RESPONDER Personalizer Whiner Sulker	**PASSIVE-AGGRESSIVE** Nag Scolder Grouch

Some answers may be circled in each box. Usually there will be more in one than another. The box that contains the most gives the general direction of your style when angry. If you fall into the "Healthy Expressive" category, congratulations! This suggests you are able to express anger, communicate your feelings, and generally let others know the anger state you are experiencing. You may have a tendency to intellectualize anger, that is, use words to defuse the emotion (yours and others'), and at times present an unsympathetic appearance.

"Emotional Responders" tend to react in terms of how they are feeling at the moment. They are likely to get their feelings hurt when anger is present in a conversation or group. This type of response often personalizes anger and sees hurt where none is intended.

115

The "Violent Responder" style is aggressive and hurtful. Acting out anger and rage is dangerous and hurts others. If you have a majority of responses in this box, additional help such as professional assessment could be useful.

If your answers fall into the "Passive-Aggressive" category, you may be the type who gets even. While you may appear to submit in the face of anger, you may get even with the person on some later occasion by being late for a meeting or missing a deadline.

Remember that we are human beings, not humanoids. Anger is a normal emotion and serves to protect us. If your style is successful, observe and reflect. If you feel anger, either violent or pent-up, it is interfering with your goals and happiness in relationships; you must take back your peace of mind.

EIGHT

HAZARDOUS TO YOUR HEALTH

*"The greatest opportunity to fix bullying or
harassment would be with the bystanders.
There are many more bystanders than there are
bullies and victims."*
Jerry Misik

More than business is conducted inside the walls of the workplace. The company is similar to a contained city or neighborhood, and has many of the same concerns: crime, violence, health hazards, harassment, troubled people, and employment issues. Businesses spend millions of dollars on these issues in the hope of arriving at solutions that will in the end save them billions.

Workers expect to receive protection and assistance from the company in times of work-related trouble. Conversely, the company expects us to do our job, act as well-mannered adults, and abide by the rules. Sounds like a fair agreement? It is. Both sides should be doing their best to keep that agreement. Watch television or read the newspaper, and you know that harassment of employees continues, hazardous fumes fill a downtown building, a berserk employee runs amok. Drugs and alcohol have yet to be eliminated from the job site. The good news is that organizations are becoming more aware of and alert to problems and are finding solutions. But nothing takes the place of personal responsibility for our health, safety, and fitness. Each individual, each employee must hunt down alternatives and remedies for job issues that affect their physical and emotional wellness.

The company is your neighborhood. Workers move in and stay for a week or a lifetime. Workers move out, some with severance pay envelopes in their hands. Others are seeking higher-paying jobs and greener pastures. Often our personal and professional lives are so intertwined, our sense of self-worth so dependent on career, that it's hard to be objective about what we're doing, where we're going, what's happening, and who's in control.

THE LINE IN THE SAND

A typical scene from *The Office* shows Toby Flenderson, HR Manager, and Michael Scott, Regional Manager, in a heated discussion of sexual harassment in the workplace following an employee's abrupt resignation. Toby states, ". . . [C]orporate asked me to do a 20-minute review of the sexual harassment policy. It's really not a big deal."

Michael replies, "IT IS A BIG DEAL! What are we supposed to do? Scrutinize every little thing we say and do all day? I mean C'mon . . . . No! They are bringing in a lawyer! What is a lawyer going to come in and tell us? Not to send out hilarious emails! Not to tell jokes? There is no such thing as an inappropriate joke. That is why it is a joke." He then went on to tell just such a joke: "A guys goes to a five-dollar lady of the night, and he gets crabs, so the next day he goes back to complain and the woman says, 'Hey, it was only five dollars. What did you expect, lobster?'" Viewers laugh at the wildly distasteful innuendo.

But in real life, many women and men would have been offended by the remark. Was it harassment? Was there real damage done? Obviously Michael didn't think so. Harassment, whether it is sexual or emotional, is hurtful and threatening. It affects mental and physical health, work performance, reputation, career moves. However, some incidents, like Michael's infamous "that's what she said" jokes, are simply annoyances. You can take control and see that it does not continue.

Shannon is a married woman and has been an insurance agent for fifteen years. "Mr. Wayland and I occupied adjacent desks in the same office space with no walls or doors separating us. For a number of months, Mr. Wayland and I were the only two employees in the office. He was my supervisor. Eventually, Mr. Wayland was able to hire a secretary and a number of new agents. At no time during the fifteen months I worked with him did he ever touch me in an inappropriate way. On the other hand, I did observe a number of occasions when he caressed his new secretary, Anita, in what appeared to be improper ways. Mr. Wayland would put his arm around her, hug her, or come up behind her while she was working on her computer and rub her shoulders. I did not hear Anita complain or ask him to stop. I don't think she encouraged him, but merely tolerated his behavior.

"It invariably surprised me how often he spent time with the female audit staff and how rarely, if ever, the discussion related to our job. Mr. Wayland commonly told dirty jokes in the presence of his female staff members with a "that's what she said," Michael Scott kind of blatancy. I did not complain to anyone because these kinds of jokes generally do not personally offend me, provided they aren't directed at a specific person.

"The fifteen months I worked for Mr. Wayland were clearly the most stressful and unproductive months of my career. My experience had me disheartened and doubting my abilities and self-worth through a series of events caused by him. For example, Mr. Wayland consistently blamed me, his secretary, Anita, and the other agents for events that had gone wrong when reporting results to our main headquarters. On occasions when Mr. Wayland would run out of people to blame for his mistakes, he would simply distort the truth.

"One day he came to my desk and advised me that he had met my former supervisor, Ms. Meyers, at a district meeting. Evidently Ms. Meyers had introduced herself as my previous boss, and Mr. Wayland responded, 'Ms. Meyers, that's not something to be proud of!' When he told me this anecdote I felt really hurt. When I expressed my irritation with his remark, he said he was just kidding. I had my doubts. I think it was his way of avoiding confrontation over his remarks—choosing to put me down to avoid "manning up."

"During the short time I had worked for him, I gained over thirty pounds. I really believe the weight gain was stress-related. And to make matters worse, he made numerous remarks about my weight gain. One time, I recall, I was hurrying to the elevator just as the doors were closing, and I heard Mr. Wayland, who was already on the elevator car, remark to the others that it was a good thing I missed the elevator because there was a weight limit. Other times he would say things to me such as, 'Lady, you're about to pop out of that dress,' suit, blouse, or whatever I happened to be wearing. My weight gain was a particular source of embarrassment to me, and it hurt to have him pointing out the ramifications of my extra pounds. On more occasions that I can list, Mr. Wayland told me if I had not been hired before he came on board, I wouldn't be working there. And his phone conversations to other agents were laced with remarks like, 'Let's talk sex!' or 'I love you too,' or 'You're so beautiful you make my day.'

"Phone messages are vital to the performance of my work. One day I phoned one of my biggest accounts and I could sense he was irritated. 'Shannon!' The client sounded annoyed and surprised. 'Why haven't you returned my phone calls? I've left several messages for you.'

"I hung up and went directly to the receptionist. Her reply to my inquiry about my messages was, 'Oh, Mr. Wayland asked me to give him all your messages.'

"That did it. I made an appointment with the company clinician through the EAP. After hearing my litany of grievances he directed me to the person who could and would give me the help I so desperately needed."

WHO'S AT FAULT HERE?

Shannon had been damaged. This was harassment. But what of Anita, Mr. Wayland's secretary? She went along with his behavior. She appeared to enjoy the hugs, the neck rubs. His off-color stories made her laugh, and his gossiping filled the gap in an otherwise boring day. The remainder of the staff thought Mr. Wayland a "good ol' boy." They had a fun group. What was the harm? Why not take the rap for Mr. Wayland from time to time when he screwed up? It was no big deal—perhaps just an annoyance.

Mr. Wayland was a liar and unprofessional, at best. He got away with his outrageous behavior because the vast majority of his staff allowed it. They too were unprofessional. Shannon had made a wise move to consult with her company EAP, and probably could have addressed her issues much sooner.

IT'S PERSONAL

Earl had been concerned about Bonita for some time. He thought to himself, *What is with her lately?* He began to have suspicions that she wasn't telling the truth about her absences from work. She claimed she had the flu twice in the last few weeks. She had been coming back late from lunch, and she looked like hell. Her sales had been dropping drastically.

Earl reflected back to the day he met Bonita. "We were both filling out our employment applications, each of us hoping to be hired as a sales representative for a major car dealership. I began a conversation with her as we waited to be called in for our interviews.

"We discovered we had a great deal in common. We had both attended the same high school. I had been a few years ahead of her class, and we had several mutual friends and acquaintances. We swapped stories in the waiting room and in general had a good time. Bonita is a cute 23-year-old redheaded chatterbox with a great sense of humor. I was sure she would make a dynamite salesperson. Well, we were both hired that day and began training the following week. Bonita excelled. Her endless energy and go-get-'em attitude turned what could have been a tedious training into fun. On the last day of our class, at the end of the day, Bonita couldn't contain herself. 'Let's get out of here and celebrate with a drink. I know a place in town where they serve doubles at half-price during happy hour.' I agreed and off we went. When we arrived I headed for an empty table. Bonita insisted we sit at the bar. She knew the bartender, Brett, and introduced us. Well, when Bonita had finished her second drink I was still working on my first. 'Wow, you're really putting those away' I told her, but she ignored my comment and ordered her third drink. I drove her home.

"On the way home Bonita told me why she had left her first job. She said women in the office were jealous of her. They gossiped and told lies about her to her sales manager. They went so far as to say she was stealing their clients. She laughed, saying that she was the best thing that ever happened to that company. She took most of the client list with her when she left. During the conversation she also told me she had just broken up with her boyfriend. They had been together two years. 'But that's okay. People always leave me; I'm used to it.' I figured it was the liquor talking."

A few weeks later, a smiling Bonita rushed into Earl's office. "Hi, Earl! What's up? What are you thinking about? Are you a million miles away?"

"Bonita," Earl replied, "You're late. Look at you, your face! Where did you get those bruises?" Bonita just laughed, "Oh, that . . . it's nothing! I just slipped and banged myself on the table as I was falling."

"Bonita," Earl said. "We have to talk." He took her by the hand and led her to an empty office. "Look," he said, "I like you and I've been concerned with your actions. Something is not right. What's bothering you?"

Bonita looked down at her feet and hesitantly began a litany of her personal problems. Her boyfriend had come back and then left her again. Both her mother, who had always pressured her to make something of herself, and her sister were not speaking to her. And her car was in the shop again. "You don't understand," she said. "My life is falling apart."

Earl felt sorry for his friend. He himself lived with his brother, a recovering alcoholic and a member of Alcoholics Anonymous for ten years now. Earl had a pretty good idea of what was happening to Bonita. "Bonita," he said, "You can't hide it any longer. As your friend I have to talk to you. Your actions have made it obvious that you have a problem, a severe one at that. Your job performance has been seriously impacted. I want to help you if you'll let me."

Bonita started to cry. "Oh no," she said, "you're just like the rest of them. You hate me too."

Earl held firm. "No, Bonita, that's not it. Remember the way you insulted Mr. Costa's wife at the awards dinner? How about the time you threw the wine at Martin Fuller just because he teased you about not having a date? Your sales are falling through the floor, nobody gets the flu as much as you do, and especially not always on a Monday."

Bonita continued to cry. "I know I drink too much. I've tried to stop. I want to. I just can't. Earl, please don't tell anyone."

"Bonita, I won't; that's up to you, but you need to know that other employees are already aware. And morale has been affected. I have a plan. Together we'll get you some help. I'll go with you to see Mr. Costa and you can tell him what you are going to do."

Mr. Costa, the general manager, invited them into the office. "Something the matter?" he asked after looking at Bonita's face.

"Well, sir, Bonita has something she would like to explain to you, and I'm here to give her some support." Through her tears Bonita confessed her problem. Mr. Costa heard her out. "Bonita, first let me tell you that I admire your courage for taking this action. The company will stand behind you, and I will check out your health insurance to see if it will cover some or all of your recovery costs. In any event, your job will be waiting for you and this conversation will remain confidential."

"Mr. Costa," Bonita asked, "are you mad at me?" He looked directly at her and said, "Bonita, if you came into the office with a broken arm would I be mad at you? It's the same thing. You're my employee, and you need medical attention. The sooner the better."

WARNING SIGNS

Smoking isn't the only thing that can be hazardous to your health. Toxic fumes can ruin more than your day. Laws are passed to protect us against toxic air, and if it happens in your workplace, get out. Don't wait until you throw up or your head feels like it will burst. There is no need to be a martyr.

A few years ago, Naomi worked in an office that was located in a commercial building occupied by several medical labs. Shortly after moving into the building, several employees began complaining about what they thought was foul-smelling air in the office. They said it smelled like formaldehyde. Naomi noticed it too. They turned down the air conditioning in an effort to stop the odor. Some of the workers said it gave them a headache. Naomi was nauseated and complained to her manager. He said he didn't notice the smell and that maybe it was the new carpeting.

Naomi insisted something needed to be done. Weeks passed with daily complaints. In an attempt to placate the workforce, management arranged to have the ventilation system checked out by representatives from the Occupational Safety and Health Administration (OSHA). The OSHA representatives found the system up to standard. But Naomi refused to give up. She knew if she let herself and her concerns be discounted that anger and resentment would only compound her discomfort.

Naomi decided to try the chief financial officer. She reasoned that the money manager might see more of the big picture. She was right. Her self-confidence and esteem were significantly boosted.

If you perceive there are unsafe conditions on your job, don't let yourself be just another complainer. Don't wait until you or your coworkers end up in a hospital. Create action steps and assert your rights to a safe and healthy workplace.

THE STALKER

Caroline, a branch manager for a government agency, was responsible for eighteen field employees. She was in charge of reviewing their caseloads and monitoring their progress. It was her duty to oversee all aspects of performance. The group was a mixed bunch. She had the usual disciplinary problems: most about the use of the phones for personal calls, a few who wasted time chatting, and some sloppy casework. Nothing she couldn't handle. The lone exception was Ernest Walker. Something was different about him. She had the strong feeling he disliked her, although he never said it.

Ernest was a well-dressed, good-looking man. He was articulate and came across as intelligent. Earnest was also a loner. Working hours began at 8:00 A.M. Ernest would come in at 8:30. When Caroline confronted him on his tardiness he replied, "I work my eight hours. I don't leave before 5:30. What's the big deal? Why can't I come in at eight-thirty?" He didn't seem to get it. The office hours were 8:00 to 5:00.

Several times during the day, Caroline would catch him staring at her. Their offices were opposite each other, Caroline's enclosed in glass, his, an open cubicle facing hers. He gave her the creeps. Performance evaluations were a part of Caroline's job. Ernest had been evaluated periodically, like her other employees. These evaluations were a way to find solutions and areas for improvement. Ernest viewed his as a threat.

It was that time again, and Caroline was not looking forward to it. Ernest sat before her as she explained the issues at hand, including his lack of performance. He stood up and began to minimize his own problems and accountability. Then he just blew up at her. "You're out to get me and I'm not going to let you get away with it!" he shouted, turned on his heel and stalked out of her office.

Caroline immediately reported the incident in writing to her branch chief. The week passed uneventfully. The following Monday one of the clerks in the building came to her office and said that on Saturday morning Ernest had been in the office, which was odd. He never came in on Saturdays. The clerk said that Ernest sat opposite Caroline's office, pointing his finger like a gun and pulling the imaginary trigger at Caroline's chair. The clerk heard Ernest saying, "Pow! Pow!"

Caroline was scared. She used every method she knew to guard herself against a physical attack, but it never came. That didn't quell her fear. She took a week's vacation to calm her nerves. Ernest was given a fitness-for-duty examination, found fit, and transferred to another division. Caroline chose to use the services of a therapist to help her work through her feelings of fear. She only wished that she could have compelled Ernest to seek help. She worried he would transfer his stalking to another woman.

Violence in the workplace has become a leading cause of workplace death for women. Document and report any fears or suspicions no matter how silly they seem. Note that Caroline informed her boss in writing, but failed to convey the fear she felt. As a supervisor, she could have referred Ernest to the company's EAP based on his tardiness, insubordination, and other job performance problems. She also could have proceeded with the first step in a disciplinary process. Furthermore, she could have asked her boss or a representative from human resources to sit in on the performance review. By handling the situation alone, Caroline subjected herself to greater fear, a wasted vacation, and severe emotional distress.

When faced with any hazard, occupational or human, it is wise to look for as many resources and supporters as possible. Don't feel it is a sign of weakness to ask for help. The daily occurrence of new and more bizarre hazards makes your responsibilities to yourself even greater.

TIME TO LEAVE?

Vanessa, an attorney, had been thinking about leaving the firm for some time. She felt her talents were unappreciated, and she couldn't envision a future with the law office she had joined eight years ago. She once had high hopes that she would someday become a partner with the law firm Mason and Mason. Even though she knew there was a "glass ceiling," Vanessa thought she could take control, crack it, and become the first female partner. She worked smart and hard, winning more than her share of tough cases.

Milt Carpenter, a sharp man and even sharper lawyer, had been awarded the partnership that Vanessa believed she had deserved. She agreed that he was good. However, her overall performance was better. Sure, Vanessa knew that Milt played handball with the younger Mr. Mason, and their wives often lunched together. Once when attending a charity, she had seen the four of them sharing the same table. The message was clear. The boys club was at it again.

It galled her that she had told the Masons of her desire to become a partner. They were kind, condescending, and said they would give careful attention to her request. "What do I have to accomplish to become a partner?" she asked. She wanted specifics. When she pressed her request to Mr. Mason, she was told that he had more important issues at hand. "We'll take it up later." Suddenly Carpenter was a full partner. She was angry. Being passed over was not only a blow to her ego but also her career.

"After the years I've given to this company, I can't believe I've been pushed aside by this handball-playing jerk, Carpenter." Now he was a jerk. Vanessa began to laugh, "I sound like a jealous ex-wife!" Vanessa knew she was a talented lawyer and other firms would be happy to have her. She acknowledged to herself that assertiveness was not her strong suit personally. But in court she was persuasive and aggressive. Recalling her conversations over the partnership, she had been wishy-washy, waiting diligently for her superior to notice her achievements. *No*, she decided, *I won't resign. I'm going after the next partnership. As a matter of fact, I'll go to Mr. Mason now. We'll negotiate.*

Thinking things out, taking responsibility for your part, and seeing the humorous side can have excellent results in your coping with hazards of any form. You may not be able to choose your boss, but you have the right to make a lot of other choices. Know that hazards exist in the workplace, just like they do in the community. When and if you encounter people or situations that might harm you, remember that there are people who can help. Use them. When seeking help for a situation that you consider makes the workplace hazardous for you, prepare and rehearse.

Then do the following:

- When you plan to talk, suggest an early, before-working hours meeting, for fewer interruptions. Make a clear statement of the meeting's importance.
- Begin with a positive statement, brief and sincere: "I appreciate how much responsibility you've given me," "Since I've been working with you, I've learned a lot about . . . ." or "Thank you for the opportunity." Remember "You always give me good advice" is a great way to start out. These are just a few of the many positive beginnings.
- Don't whine, complain, blame, or bring in others. "My husband doesn't like . . . my therapist says . . . my

children need . . ." are all no-no's. Stand on your own two feet.

- In line with avoiding negativity don't blame the person you are talking to for the problem. Do not criticize the boss; instead, praise, praise, praise.
- Remember to show the benefits for remedying the situation. You're selling a product or service.
- Be clear. Define the issues that are really important to you. Beforehand examine your own motives. Do you truly want to improve working conditions? Facts and support will be available when you have diagnosed a real problem.
- After the meeting send your boss a thank-you note. Don't wait for his or her action. You are expressing thanks for time and listening.
- What if nothing changes? Disappointment doesn't mean failure. The success is in the constructive confrontation, taking the risk. The meeting was not the end product, only one step. Keep moving.
- No employee is required to take abuse or be subjected to health hazards. Do not be bullied, discounted, or intimidated. At the same time stand up for yourself. Don't blame or invalidate others.

> *"Much of what we experience in the workplace is not fair; we shouldn't have to work in an environment that violates our integrity and self-esteem. But life itself is not always fair.*
> *The key is learning how to get our needs met in an unfair system."*
> Diane Tracy

All too frequently job satisfaction is linked to our unrealistic expectations about what the job can provide. We invest our entire selves, our time, energy, health, and family happiness. What can we expect to receive in return that will reward us for such a sacrifice? We must have more realistic expectations and balance our contribution and effort with requirements.

Take It Back

Recognize

1. Make a list of hazards that affect you on the job. Include human ones.
2. Keep a diary of events in the office that may be suspect. Discard annoyances.
3. Recognize your feelings. Have you been concerned, harboring resentments, or feeling anxious and afraid?

Respond

1. What is one thing that I can do to correct a bad situation? (e.g., Simply writing in a journal is an action step)
2. What am I waiting for? (The right time?) How long am I willing to wait?
3. Are there risks in taking a next step?
4. Evaluate your concerns, consider another opinion, and then take them to someone who can do something about them. Remember to follow up.

Reinforce

1. Choose the affirmation that fits your situation:
   - My opinions and questions are valid. I have the right to a response.
   - I can say no!
   - I can drop this matter, forgive those involved, and deflect the situation. I practice patience and tolerance.

- I am as important as anyone else in this company. I am a valuable employee.
- I will teach others how to treat me. I deserve courtesy. I deserve respect.
- I have the power to direct my life, my career, and my health.

2. Determine the next steps in addressing hazards. Decide that the situation is important to you. Know that you and other persons you wish to defend have been genuinely mistreated or exposed. Commit to assertive action.

3. Know that you can repeat or escalate your actions. You can state the consequences of continuing hazardous conditions. Make notes about how you can proceed with assertiveness.

NINE

Ethical Dilemma

> *"The happy, expansive life is not a life free of*
> *adversity nor a life spent in contented leisure.*
> *Rather, it is the life of accomplishment, learning*
> *and growth."*
> Frederick G. Harmon

Often employee stress stems from unethical moral or political intrusion in the workplace. Whether name-calling or harassment, an affair between boss and coworker, or lying about delivery dates, an employee faced with contradictions to a personal value system is a conflict. How can an individual in a frustrating and seemingly no-win situation evaluate these conflicts wisely and take appropriate action? How can an employee deal with the inner turmoil created by the actions of others? Individuals within companies, representatives of companies, and corporations themselves all operate within an ethical, moral, and political framework.

Whether the source of a moral, ethical, or political dilemma is within the corporate structure or just the idiosyncratic behavior of one person, the employee who is offended by the condition surrounding work, or even faced with serious consequences, will be undermined. Taken a step further, the offensive situation can have serious and even legal consequences if ignored. How can an individual in such a ticklish situation set boundaries, evaluate consequences of action (or inaction) wisely, and balance personal values and beliefs with the realities of the workplace? Practical ways of dealing with ethical and political realities are an important part of surviving with your job and self-esteem intact.

THE WOLF IN BOSS'S CLOTHING

Cynthia worked in a biomedical corporation that prided itself on flexibility in meeting employees' needs. Though her salary was low, the childcare benefits were very high, and she could work a flex-time schedule. She and her husband had worked out a complex but efficient schedule for caring for their two-year-old son and nine-month-old daughter. As a data analyst, she worked independently of others and came in two nights per week from 9:00 to 11:00 P.M. Usually she was alone in the office with an occasional visit from one of the security guards who knew her well.

Getting ready to leave one night, she was quietly gathering up her things when she heard the security locks in the outer office being turned. She heard laughter and giggling. Startled, she stood listening. To her shock she realized the vice president of marketing was speaking to a woman who was clearly not his wife. The couple went down the hall into his private office and closed the door. She could still hear laughter and glasses clinking. To her further shock she realized the female voice belonged to Reba, a researcher from the lab. Mortified at overhearing this rendezvous, Cynthia quickly and quietly left the building. She alternately wished for and feared meeting a security guard.

As she drove home Cynthia was angry, shocked, and overwhelmed. She was personally offended that a married man, and a boss, would be so blatant in carrying on an affair, especially at the office. She felt anger and sympathy for Reba, who would no doubt be the one to suffer if this indiscretion was found out. Then she began to think about herself. Should she report this? What would she say? Could she just ignore what was going on? What if this continued? Could she work after hours without running into the scandal? Question after question began to scroll through her brain.

Cynthia was faced with a serious problem. Not only were her personal values offended by the situation in the workplace, but she felt some responsibility to protect the company. A scandal could seriously impact the company's prestige as it was currently venturing a public stock offering. The ramifications went beyond her comfort level into job security. Was there a "right" thing to do?

If she told anyone, she didn't know who it'd be. Her own boss, a stereotype of the absentminded professor, would probably not even know who or what she was talking about. They'd both be embarrassed. Should she go to the human resource director? The incident would probably come under the category of sexual harassment, and then she'd be involved and have to file a claim. Everyone would know. And Cynthia would probably be the one to incur the wrath of not only the "double agents" but also of others who sympathized with them or simply didn't like snitches or espionage. Now Cynthia began to feel like she was the one who had done something wrong.

Duties and Dilemmas

Humberto was studying to get his real estate license. He had obtained a job as a receptionist in a large and very busy real estate office. Each day prospective renters, buyers, and sellers would call for information on listings that legally required the answers to come from a licensed agent. Often the callers became angry with Humberto because he could not legally give them information they considered very simple to obtain. Callers did not understand the law and thought Humberto had the information easily at hand.

After only a few weeks, Humberto's manager, John, called him in for a review. John's praise for Humberto's few weeks on the job was effusive. Humberto was feeling great as he listened to the compliments. Then the dialogue took a detour. "You know, it might be easier if you just give out the updated listing information. You could make life easier for all of us. I know you'll pass your exam when you take it next month, and we just don't have the time to be asking agents to call these people back." John closed the meeting emphasizing teamwork and implied Humberto would quickly move up in the company by working in an expedient manner.

Returning to his desk, Humberto sat quietly, mindlessly turning a pencil in his hand. The impact of what John was asking of him gradually filled him with anxiety. Yet John had made the request sound so simple and logical. Clearly he didn't feel any anxiety around his request of Humberto. Both Cynthia and Humberto faced situations characterized by moral, political, and ethical complexities. While Cynthia's situation did not include behavior condoned by the corporation, as did Humberto's, both situations posed potentially serious consequences no matter what action the employee took.

DEGREE OF DISSONANCE

The first step in dealing with a moral and ethical dilemma is to be clear about your own value system and to examine your own motivation. Cynthia began to think along these lines. She was surprised to find her thoughts straying to the executive's wife. She realized that her strong opinions about infidelity had never surfaced before. She wondered if she was projecting how she might feel if her husband, Scott, was unfaithful. Cynthia began to picture the vice president standing in front of a large executive desk with his head hanging low, being lectured by the president of the company, then rushing home with roses to surprise his loving wife. She realized the scene would more realistically resemble the "old boys' club" or a locker room with herself as the butt of the jokes as the executive asked the vice president to be more discreet and take his affair to a motel where it belonged.

Humberto was thinking too. As he evaluated his situation he found himself worrying more about being caught than about the legality of what he was being asked to do. He was surprised at his own willingness to evaluate the risks rather than to simply refuse. He was disappointed in himself as he equivocated in his thinking.

Both Humberto and Cynthia are evaluating the degrees of dissonance they are experiencing. Each situation contained choices that produced a range of feelings: anger, irritation, anxiety, and fear. The situations also produced the potential for serious consequences ranging from legal ramifications in the real estate office to simple embarrassment for Cynthia. Both knew that to some extent reporting, in Cynthia's case, and refusing, in Humberto's, would reduce the discomfort, the level of dissonance, and stress. But action would create a new level of discomfort in other areas. Certainly it seemed Humberto would be fired either way, and Cynthia would have to consider the worst case scenario of upsetting her delicately balanced childcare schedule.

In the workplace, dilemmas of this nature can simply be irritating. Others can be dangerous and deadly. Cynthia finally made a decision. She decided to consult with the personnel manager. She was risking that her confidence might be abused and the story become office gossip, but she knew that she had to take the risk in order to reduce the level of discomfort she was feeling. The stress had now become severe and her preoccupation with the situation debilitating. She seemed to develop a headache every time she thought about the situation.

Humberto felt similar distress and decided to try talking with John to express his feelings of discomfort. He also presented a way of grouping phone calls so that one agent could handle all the renters and another deal with the buyers and sellers. Humberto was prepared to be fired or resign if John pressed him to violate the real estate regulations.

In both situations, Humberto and Cynthia had become very stressed and found that an action step, regardless of the consequences, was necessary to restore their peace in going about the daily tasks of living and working. Luckily, both received a positive response. John accepted Humberto's ideas and said no more about the situation. Humberto planned to give the real estate company at least six months of hard work and then look for another job. He felt that the company's ethics would come into conflict with his own value system and goals in the future.

Cynthia was assured that her confidence would be respected and was told that the situation had already come to the attention of the president of the company and was being addressed. When, nine months later, Cynthia learned of the vice president's promotion and transfer, she was disappointed but realized that business demands had probably dictated a compromise. She could live with the corporate decision. Cynthia and Humberto won their own internal conflicts.

Selling Your Ideas

As you begin to take action steps to assert yourself, change job conditions, or influence the behavior of those around you, it pays to follow the rules of successful salespeople. You are trying to sell yourself and your ideas. An important part of any sale is creating a belief that your idea will help the other person achieve his or her own goals. Begin with the idea that you are here to provide ideas that complement the department's or company's objectives. Do your homework, be specific, and cite examples. Again, emphasize benefit. I know that if you can resolve this, there will be some positive results in productivity. In Humberto's story he balanced his refusal with a positive suggestion.

Rehearse your pitch with another person. If the situation has happened with other employees, and they have successfully resolved it, cite them as endorsements. Be specific about the role you would like the boss to play: "When you speak with me, I'd like you to lower your voice, and not call me names." "When you overload me with conflicting demands I become confused. Can you help by giving me only one direction at a time?"

But what if you've tried working with your boss and have reached a dead end? You can honestly say that you've done everything you can. Perhaps substance abuse, anger, or personality conflicts have pushed the situation beyond that which assertive communication can address.

Lethal Leapfrog

Going over your boss's head can be a dangerous tactic. It is important to assess what is at stake. Is the issue worth the risk? Assess the degree of discomfort you are feeling. Your judgments and values have brought you into conflict with a person or a policy. Now, how serious is the dilemma? First, evaluate the actual damage to you personally. Are you irritated, embarrassed, or inconvenienced? These conditions certainly can be stressful but may not be worth risking your political standing or your future.

Take the damage estimate a step further. Does this really affect you directly? Notice in Cynthia's situation she was not directly affected. Another individual might have been able to ignore the situation. Discuss your "damage vs. risk" ratio with others. Be open to the possibility that you have over- or underestimated the damage or the risks. In the following story you may be surprised at an employee's response to measurable damage. Have a strategy before beginning your campaign.

Teacher's Pet

Vic and Maila worked for Progressive Savings and Loan before its collapse and eventual takeover by the Resolution Trust Corporation. From her first day of employment Maila could see that their boss, Heather, had given Vic preferred treatment. Since Vic and Maila were loan officers, they were assigned company vehicles that they were able to use for commuting as well as business. When a new car became available, Vic got first choice. Heather seemed to funnel walk-in customers to Vic. Since both Vic and Maila were paid commission based on the number of commercial loans they brought into the bank, the favoritism seemed obvious and unfair.

Rumors circulated that Heather and Vic had been seen kissing after an office holiday party a couple of years back. In fact, it seemed that most men working for Heather were treated better than the women. Maila could readily see that Heather's biases were creating a problem. Malia was increasingly angry and resentful. She had begun complaining to all her friends. She knew it was time to address the problem but was unsure of a next step. If she confronted Heather with her observations, Heather would not accept the truth. If she went over Heather's head, the consequences were unpredictable. If she tried and failed, her own reputation was at stake.

Maila knew that she would always get second choice in cars and customers and make less money than Vic as long as this went on. It was frustrating, but not life-threatening. Maila knew she could look for another job, but she liked her coworkers and the benefits were good. Further, Maila did not like change. So, she decided to keep her concerns to herself. She began to address the resentment she felt by reframing. Gradually she was able to change her attitude from negative resentment to positive acceptance. Her self-talk included statements like, "I'm learning a lot about being a manager, and I see my own biases by watching others."

To her pleasant surprise Vic was offered a better job with another Savings and Loan and left the company. Heather and Maila then began to get along better and worked as partners. Maila realized Heather was not biased against women. The situation resolved itself through the passing of time.

Did you have a different idea of what Maila's response should have been? Try to measure the potential for achieving a positive result before you take action. This story presents a case history in which accepting a very problematic situation had a positive outcome. Another approach might have worked equally well. Not every situation is immediately solvable nor is there only one correct response. The "right" way is measured by the degree of ease and relief from distress you gain from your action.

Later, after the Resolution Trust Corporation underwent closings and restructurings, Maila and Heather both found themselves looking for work. Heather found a job almost immediately and recommended the company hire Maila. Maila certainly profited by maintaining a good working relationship with her boss even when things were not going her way. Now Maila received the dividends earned by her patience.

If you have made an assessment that you must go over the boss's head to get help in resolving a problem, you might be successful. If you don't act, the damage to working relationships could be serious. While most companies have a procedure for going over the supervisor's head, the action threatens the corporate chain of command. Your boss's superiors must—in a confrontation—back your boss. Further, leapfrogging can make you suspect with your peers and also at odds with your own supervisor. The tactic may give you the reputation with upper management as a troublemaker. Remember, assess real damage, the degree of dissonance, and look at possible outcomes and consequences before you choose this strategy.

But what if your boss is an obstacle, a pain in the neck, totally unworkable, and unreasonable? Run through this checklist first.

1. Break your ideas up into small segments. For example, rather than discussing "our communication" or "my job," you can give the boss bite-size pieces for digestion. Speak slowly and in short sentences. Wait for a response before moving on. Provide him or her an outline of your suggestion for later review.

2. Try to ease into an attitude of acceptance rather than fighting. For example, "I really want to do this correctly," and "I am uncomfortable with being less than candid. I want to assist you. I can (state the

acceptable behavior)." If the outcome of your efforts is still unsuccessful or unacceptable, you can feel good about yourself for trying one more possible avenue for resolution. You've done all you can at that level.

MIRROR, MIRROR

Very often we don't realize that we can be our own worst enemy. Several good indicators are the way we treat others, how others treat us, what our surroundings look like, and how we care for and treat ourselves. When we feel mistreated by ourselves or others, it is often easier to blame and criticize than look at our own part in creating a bad situation. Perhaps we create problems or see them where none actually exist. Low self-esteem is frequently associated with negative and critical attitudes. This simple quiz, answered honestly, will serve as a measure of your relationship with yourself, and probably with others. Answer yes or no to the following questions:

1. Are you verbally abusive?
2. Are you physically abusive?
3. Do you often find yourself saying, "I'm sorry"?
4. Do you allow anyone to verbally assault you?
5. Does anyone physically abuse you?
6. Do you make excuses for other people's behavior?
7. Do you seek approval of your personal appearance?
8. Are your friends smarter than you?
9. Are your friends better looking than you?
10. Do you seek friends' opinions before changing your hairstyle?
11. Do you keep attracting losers in your personal as well as professional life?
12. Do you feel like a victim?
13. Do you put other people down?
14. Do you frequently gossip?

15. Do you always need a reason for what you do?
16. Do you usually need help in making decisions?
17. Do you feel you have to justify your behavior to others?
18. Can other people's opinions ruin your day?
19. Are you overly generous? Do you frequently give more than you get?
20. Do you make fun of yourself in a deprecating way?
21. Do you brag?
22. Do you need other people's approval?
23. Do you reject assistance?
24. Are you unhappy with your life?
25. Do you feel guilty?
26. Does life frighten you?
27. Does change upset you?
28. Are you fearful of trying something new?
29. Is your car in constant disrepair?
30. Do you avoid checkups with your dentist?
31. Do you put off medical examinations?
32. Is your closet cluttered?

SCORING: Count the number of "yes" answers.

1 to 5	I feel pretty good about myself!
6 to 12	I could use some uplifting.
13 and above	It's time to do some work on my self-esteem.

Now look at the patterns. The answers to each number correlate with these categories to give a label to the behavior that needs attention.

Anger Management: Items 1, 2, 4, 5, 25, 26

Self-Esteem: Items 8, 9, 10, 22, 29, 30, 32

Self-Confidence: Items 7, 8, 9, 13, 14, 15, 16, 17, 21, 28, 30

Codependence: Items 3, 6, 11, 12, 18, 19, 23, 24, 27

When a behavior change needs to occur, move rapidly to address the problem. Check local adult education or college extension programs for courses and workshops addressing anger management or self-esteem. Consider individual assessment with a professional therapist. Investigate free self-help groups like Codependents Anonymous.

ARSENAL OF WORDS

Being specific is critical in increasing personal power. Regardless of the nature of your dilemma—moral, political, ethical, or a combination of many—simply documenting the situation and circumstances is an action step. Documentation provides an accurate base for developing a next step, should the situation continue or arise again. Too often in the workplace the term "document" is applied only to negative situations with an implied threat of some future whistleblowing. Yet the habit of documenting can be a very positive one.

For example, relate this to performance reviews. Many employees are disappointed, even surprised, at the results of their yearly or biannual performance reviews. For many, the longest week of the year culminates in a lead-footed march into the boss's office for a performance review. Even the most competent and self-assured worker can be rattled by the unknown in these situations. It is normal to hear criticism. Yet these reviews are structured by the company to provide feedback, both positive and negative aspects of employee performance.

By preparing for performance reviews you can create a forum for assertive communication. Such preparation includes adequate documentation. Most employees simply make the "death march" and sit listening in dread or with eventual relief. However, these reviews are not just about you. They simply represent your manager's view of your performance, the corporate process, biased rating systems, and company policies, both fair and unfair (e.g., "This company never gives 'excellents.' If it did, what would you be striving for?").

First, envision this review as a time when you have an uninterrupted opportunity to influence your boss. Prepare for this chance by keeping track of regular discussions with your supervisor, taking notes, and maintaining them in a current and timely fashion. Your memos to yourself should note compliments as well as criticisms. Make sure that any criticism is corrected and that you have brought that correction to your boss's attention, having made a note of the date of the discussion.

Keep a list of your achievements, no matter how small. Record when you have exceeded an expectation, worked on a special team, gone beyond your job description, or completed work before deadlines. Quote compliments you have received from others. To make this simple, keep just one file. Drop little notes, even scribbles, into it. Don't wait until you have time to document or write yourself a memo. The rule here is to do it now, no matter what the form.

Taking Charge

Before your scheduled performance meeting get a copy of the review form to be used. Complete this review of yourself. Try and be tough as well as objective. This may help you structure your notes and lists of achievements. Put them in the appropriate section to document your rating or the ideas that you want to "sell" to the boss.

Then, expect the negative. Remember, most evaluations by definition include the negative. Most bosses feel a review is balanced only if it includes negative comments. If you anticipate the negative you may be less surprised and resentful of it. Make sure that at the conclusion of the review you receive behavioral objectives for the next period. Don't let the boss get away with vague comments like, "Improve your attitude," or "You need more technological skills." As a rule of thumb, you should be able to draw a picture of anything that is a goal. The old rule of SMART applies here. A goal should be:

SPECIFIC
MEASURABLE
ACHIEVABLE
RELEVANT
TIMELY

"Improve your attitude" may then translate into, "Reduce your negative comments in staff meeting by 80 percent," or, "Make one positive comment in each departmental staff meeting." Even if your boss does not state your performance objectives in behavioral terms, you can do so after the review is completed. Confirm your interpretation in writing. For example, translate "Increase motivation" to "I will initiate five sales calls per day." Don't be reluctant to set goals for the boss: "As we discussed, you will meet with me monthly to discuss progress. I will initiate that meeting."

Take control of your own future by ensuring that your next review will be more productive and adequately reflect your accomplishments. Let the review process motivate you to keep better track of your own productivity. Even though the review process may be poorly designed and/or executed, take responsibility and reshape it to meet your needs.

As you read this chapter, you may find yourself saying, *Well, these are all good ideas, but I'm still not ready to take action. How can I make a decision?*

To Do or Not to Do

How do people make decisions? What is an effective decision-making process? The answers to these questions are numerous and varied. Often people avoid making decisions by simply allowing a process to take its course. A wife may deny the evidence of her spouse's affair, unconsciously allowing fate to take its course. A boss may deny the evidence of an employee's substance abuse problem, hoping that some miracle will change things. Some individuals let others make decisions for them, saying, "Whatever you want." A throw of the dice, a toss of the coin can create a decision, but you are not then a part of the process. You are, however, stuck with the consequences. Informed and effective decision making is not secret; it is simply a process of six steps.

1. First, probe for all the facts you need. In evaluating a situation it is important to get the perspectives of others. In dealing with a perplexing, abusive, or stressful job situation it is important to know your rights and that your perspective is shared by others. This may mean taking some risks, exposing vulnerability, and examining character defects in yourself. Evidence gathering is still a necessary step.

2. Next, put yourself into motion. Understand that at the conclusion of the process you will make a decision. Know that each step of the process is moving you closer to the point of decision. Envision a rolling wheel or snowball. See yourself successfully moving toward your goal.

3. Think in terms of different routes. Let alternatives emerge rather than trying to arrive at the single perfect course of action. As you share your situation with others, some will say, "Get another job." But more likely you will hear alternatives to "go or stay." Listen to the subtlety of others' suggestions to you. Reject nothing out-of-hand. Allow several alternatives to stay on your mental list, including those you might label unacceptable—"Sue the jerk!" Don't defend against perceived criticism.

4. Don't undervalue intuition. You know what is best for yourself. Often trusting ourselves is difficult. Perhaps you are juggling denial and self-acceptance. But you are a trustworthy person and you can probably believe in yourself. Your inclinations are probably on target. Listen to see if others are validating your intuitive feelings. Using a process serves to double-check intuition.

5. Make the call. This means immediately announcing the decision to others (depending on the circumstances this may be a limited few) and begin your action plan. Don't wait or you will defeat your purpose.

6. If the decision is wrong, just say, "Oops." Then start over. Admit you were wrong or that the course of action was too difficult or not realistic. Correct your course and move on.

Win-Win

In his book, *The Seven Habits of Highly Effective People,* Stephen Covey writes, "Most people have cultivated habits of ineffectiveness—blaming others, thinking selfishly, only seeking to be understood but not seeking to understand others." He goes on to say, "You must have certain positive habits to function effectively, habits that are the foundation of your character." Fortunately for us all, these habits can be learned.

Covey suggests we learn to be proactive. Choose your responses; act rather than being acted upon; begin with the end in mind. This fits in very well with visualizing the outcome, seeing how you want the picture to look when you finish. Put first things first. For all of us there are too many things to do and too little time. Remember, "No" is still a complete sentence.

EVALUATE PRIORITIES

Think win-win. There is enough of all we need for everyone. We can all prosper. Be mature and self-confident. Know that you can have what you want without diminishing anyone else. Understand—then be understood. Listen to learn, but first learn to listen. Synergize—meaning, don't be defensive. Try to open yourself to new possibilities. Finally, Covey suggests, sharpen the saw. You are the saw and must renew yourself by taking care of your mental, spiritual, emotional, and physical needs.

No organization praises or tolerates poor performance. "Ha!" you say, "Just look at my company." There is poor performance in the industry that is not confronted; often, it's swept under the rug. This is reality, not an idealized, perfect world. In order for you to be highly satisfied with your life, your job situation must be addressed. There must be constructive confrontation. This means bringing the inequities, the conflicts, and the poor performance of others out into the open. This also means using techniques, being proactive, taking control, and acting in a way that is consistent with your own value system.

Only by operating with integrity, self-esteem, good intention, and goodwill can you effectively create a change. Once you begin, you are on the path to creating a satisfying success that says, "I manage myself. I cooperate in accomplishing tasks that are given to me by others. I am my own boss, my own manager, my own best friend."

ETHICAL STANDOFF

When moral, ethical, and political dilemmas arise, you may feel that there are no choices left to you. It is not unusual to find that certain job titles and responsibilities make otherwise easygoing, good people unbearable. They begin to put so much effort into maintaining control that they become oppressive as bosses and managers. This is the supervisor who used to be a buddy and now rules with an iron fist and makes arbitrary decisions. Such an individual lets you know that he or she has a position with power. And you better not forget it. There are also corporate policies, or unspoken rules, in certain organizations that are not acceptable to you. There are times that retreat is the best choice for survival.

The major obstacle to dealing with a boss, an unacceptable attitude, or a corporate culture that you find unethical is that you will probably not be able to change the person's or group's outlook with rational argument. Don't be a crusader tilting at windmills and do not become a doormat and give up. Instead, find ways to adapt and make changes that will improve your own ability to accept this difficult situation.

If you have examined your situation exhaustively and find that you cannot adapt, there is a next step, but first refer back to Chapters Three and Four on dysfunction and personality style in the workplace. Then identify the individual or corporate personality you're dealing with. Review the suggestions for working with such type. Try to figure out the dysfunctional dynamics that are in operation. Has the boss had a tough climb up the organizational ladder? Is he or she under undue stress from certain corporate policies and practices? Whatever the cause, this is the way your boss or company is and will probably continue to be, at least in the time you have to deal with your own unease. Face this fact squarely and anticipate reactions based on past history. *That's just what I expected* can be your reaction, rather than hurt, anger, or surprise that your efforts or proposals weren't received in a more positive manner.

Pick a middle ground. No, you're not submissive, meekly kowtowing to every whim and order. Nor do you need to be the Rebel-Without-a-Clue, constantly questioning and challenging. There are too many ways bosses can win at manipulative games. Maintain your independence and know that you can take a strategic stand to fight for what is important to you. Be aware of where your moral and ethical lines are. Having decided on this more judicious path, you can go along with some distasteful actions and activities, knowing the limits you have set. Or you may have to retreat.

Find a balance between staying out of the boss's way and being visible for the success and achievements you make. Try to do everything right the first time. It may be helpful to get the opinion of another on the instructions given to you if they are vague and if it would be unwise to ask the boss for clarification. A network of information sources can be very helpful. And don't fall prey to cutting down your boss when you make these inquiries. Gossip and backbiting, no matter how satisfying at the moment, will generally backfire.

Also, learn, learn, and learn some more. Even the most objectionable and domineering boss may still be able to teach you a great deal. He or she has gotten to that position through creativity, expertise, or simply pure domination. A sincere interest in how this person is effective can help recontext your feelings. You can also learn how not to act when you are the boss. Pass on what you have learned. If your boss never praises the good work you do, go immediately to another and praise their work. Praise your spouse for simply getting up in the morning and going to work; praise your children just for being them. You learn by teaching yourself.

Use gratitude. Handwritten thank-you notes are not an out-of-date invention. Whenever successfully receiving assistance, always write a simple thank-you note or shoot off a quick text. Whether you use personalized professional stationery or your smartphone, you can't overuse this technique. Presenting this suggestion in a seminar, I was interrupted by a bright young man in a power-red tie, crisply laundered shirt, and braces who said, "I can't do that. My handwriting is atrocious." Everyone laughed and several volunteers offered to help him out.

Anyone employed by a corporation, large or small, must be realistic about what their commitments and rewards are. The famous English jurist Lord Edward Thurlow, in response to a question, once said, "Did you ever expect a corporation to have a conscience when it has no soul to be damned, and no body to be kicked?" While it is true that corporations work best when they reward, appreciate, and motivate, people nevertheless become an overhead item on a balance sheet. Without the ability to control the costs, no corporation can survive.

In these lean and mean days, the corporation is sharper than ever and even less compassionate. Managers and supervisors are as vulnerable as rank-and-file workers. Employees who are limited in their job skills and who have only one specialty are especially vulnerable. Let go of any ideas you have of corporate job security, or what the company owes you. Take an unsentimental look around you. Even if your corporation is making money or your department is doing well, there may be other operations that are failing. Take a hard look at your job. Could it be done by someone who can be paid substantially less? Would the operation suffer substantially if your job were eliminated or combined with another? What would happen to you if your boss or your mentor were fired or transferred?

Many conscientious employees, managers and line workers alike, have come to have an unrealistic view of their own importance in the corporate scheme of things. They feel that the hard work and long hours they put into getting the job done will be recognized and rewarded. They feel that each year these continuing efforts make them all the more valuable. But keep Thurlow's view in mind—a corporate entity has no feelings, no conscience, and no body that feels pain. Chief operating officers, consultants, and accountants are not likely to view the individual soul on a balance sheet.

It may be helpful to visualize where you would be if your job or operation were limited. Look at your job as if you were on *Survivor*. Then begin to explore your present possibilities. Now is the time to be political, to form alliances, to create favors (helping others creates a relationship in which they owe you, if only psychologically), or ally with a mentor. Now is the time to increase your value to the corporation by going to school, taking on additional responsibilities, and asking for greater cross-training opportunities. Teach yourself. You are still in a good position. You can give people what they want, while making sure you receive in return.

Take It Back

Recognize

Write down the fifteen most successful experiences of your life. Often people say, "a good marriage," "having children," "getting a promotion," "quitting smoking," or "building an addition to my house."

Respond

In each experience listed above, cite two or three strengths that were critical to this success. For example, "I used willpower to quit smoking and to keep on with the addition to my house," or, "It took a lot of patience to rear children and go back to school." Now look for the pattern that forms. Perhaps you have asked for help from others who've been in similar situations. This is the pattern that should be applied to solving the problems you face at work.

Reinforce

To reinforce success, use the pattern of strengths you found above. In one example, asking for help is a pattern. Use that strength in a current dilemma. Use any of these strengths and patterns alone and you'll progress. Use them together and you'll see the progress not just adding up, but multiplying!

1. Recognize your own responsibility in each situation. Did you meddle, speak out of turn, unfairly judge another, miss a deadline, or blame the computer? Adopt

the "If it is to be, it depends on me" philosophy. Act as if there is no they—only me!

2. In spite of the problems and discomfort you face, aim for a 100 percent effort. Work to the best of your ability, keeping your productivity high in spite of challenge.

3. Identify the next step up for you in the organization. Identify the skills and recommendations you will need that are essential to making the move. Begin today to make the plan, and tomorrow begin working at it. If you don't see a next promotional step, you'll have to create one.

4. Repeat the following statements at least twice a day:
    *   Today is a new opportunity.
    *   I can begin again.
    *   The past is not an excuse for my behavior.
    *   No one is stopping me.
    *   I can learn to forget.

TEN

TRANSCENDING TECHNOLOGY

"Once a man would spend a week patiently waiting
if he missed a stage coach.
Now he rages if he misses the first section of a
revolving door."
Simeon Strunsky

"We are stuck with technology when what we really
want is just stuff that works."
Douglas Adams
Author, *The Salmon of Doubt*

Downsize. Cutting edge. Automate and fast track. Partnering and outsourcing. These are just a few of the terms we overhear in today's corporate world. Texting, apps, Facebook, Skype—terms unknown a couple of decades ago are now implanted in our everyday life at the workplace.

Prior to World War II, change in America occurred gradually. Progress was steady, foreseeable, and easily integrated into acceptable mental increments. We had the luxury of doing strategic planning with some degree of certainty.

No longer. We're in an unpredictable world where technology is a whirlwind. Where will it go, our high-tech world of tomorrow? Ten years from now, every computer, every machine, every electronic process we now use will be obsolete, like much of our accepted business practices and procedures. But what about our living environments? Our cities and towns? Physically nothing has changed. Or has it?

DOWNLOAD OVERLOAD

It's not just the language we speak. Our business language must adapt too. We can't fight terms and ideas like 4G, cloud computing, Bluetooth, tablet, and 3-D printing, a revolution which is quickly gaining momentum. Keys that jangled on chains are no longer useful and have been replaced by magnetic cards or push-to-start cars. Now we get to worry that the card will get wet, demagnetized, or that our phones might run out of batteries, or worse, get lost or stolen. Faster and faster, the world as we know it is changing.

Fear of our jobs becoming obsolete is often paramount in our minds. It's happened on the assembly lines in factories all over this country. In the office, where not long ago it took five or six switchboard operators to facilitate the calls of a busy company, now there are none. The new telecommunications system handles it all. The digital voice directs us to "press five to speak to an operator." In the near future telephone operators and the neighborhood bank teller will have gone the way of miniskirts and boy bands.

Reactions to new technology have been varied. Some workers are known to have celebrated the news of a virus in the computer. Others have cursed or cried, knowing hours of research and weeks of input have vanished in a microsecond. How we survive the changes and challenges of the information age may depend on our willingness to take constructive, not destructive, actions.

THE MONKEY WRENCH

Vernon could feel the bile rising in his throat. He took another antacid and noticed that half the chips were gone. He had opened the new package only a couple of hours ago. Vernon was feeling like a salmon swimming upstream, facing rapids and frantically paddling his arms. Just as he mastered one crisis, another faced him. Last month Vernon had celebrated his 50th birthday. Today he wondered if he could make it to 51. Vernon had been employed with Bolton Inc. for almost 18 years and had been through many changes as the company grew and expanded. He had never obtained the necessary education or had the desire to enter into management. "I just don't like to give orders," he would say when asked why he didn't move up in the company.

When Vernon was hired at Bolton, all that was required of him was to show up on time, do the job, and be honest and dependable. His employment application had been on one page—name, age, address, social security number, level of education, and one reference (he gave his father-in-law). The personal interview with Mr. Bolton had been brief and ended with a firm handshake. *Good Lord*, Vernon thought. *If I wanted to get hired at Bolton today, I would never make it.* Now the personnel department occupied one whole floor. The applications are eight pages long, not including a resume, plus a mandatory drug test. Ph.D.'s are standing in line for entry-level positions. Vernon had to admit that the younger people coming on board now had a lot of smarts, especially with this new communications mumbo jumbo, which to them was second nature.

Vernon knew he was having a hard time adapting. In the past he had felt safe and comfortable with his position at Bolton. He was looking forward to his retirement at 65, to playing golf with the guys, and to spending time with Robin, his wife of more than 20 years. Now things weren't working out the way he had planned. A monkey wrench was thrown into Vernon's dream.

Old Wayne Bolton's twenty-six-year-old daughter, Taylor, had come into the company fresh out of grad school and had been handed the job of chief of operations. Vernon had known her for years, as a nice little kid who often played in the mail room or warehouse when her dad would bring her to work with him. Now, as an adult, her style was aloof and brisk. When Taylor spoke to

Vernon her language was filled with words and terminology he didn't understand. One thing had been made crystal clear: Vernon would have to get up to speed with his computer skills. He had been through the basic training when the company first shifted to automation a few years back. It was hard to learn, but in his job he didn't need to use it much. Most of his work was verbal.

Now the supervisor told the team that Taylor was introducing an entirely new system. Since that announcement, Vernon had not slept well. Robin, his wife, was nagging him about his poor eating habits and sudden outbursts of temper. He had always been a healthy and easygoing kind of guy, and he surprised himself at his recent behavior and physical discomfort. His stomach burned and his heart pounded when he thought about the new program. It featured instant messaging and group chats. When it was installed he would no longer be able to talk with his supervisor or coworkers. The new rules explained that he was not to leave his workstation. No longer could he phone them or walk to their office: he had to use email or text. Vernon was in a panic. Thoughts of quitting entered his mind. Where would he go? He couldn't compete at fifty. Giving up his pension and other benefits was out of the question. For a brief time, thoughts of suicide came into his mind.

The root of Vernon's misery lay in the fact that he had never in his adult life written a letter to anyone. Not even Robin. How could he tell anyone that secret? His coworkers respected him and now they would laugh behind his back. Vernon was actually embarrassed. His spelling skills were almost nonexistent. Why couldn't Taylor have remained the cute little girl handing out mail?

This employee is caught in a tech trap. The need for new knowledge comes faster than the mind can accommodate it. No wonder we resent new technology; discomfort is the byproduct. We feel lost somewhere in the middle of the information highway.

Vernon took the highroad. Mustering all his courage, he went directly to Taylor's office. She listened intently as Vernon swallowed his shattered pride and disclosed his secret. Finally, she answered. "Oh, is that all you're concerned about? No problem. Our local community college has some courses you can attend in the evening, at very low cost. It's my understanding that they feature a class in business letter composition. Also there are some very good books on the subject. One book that helped me was *How to Say It* by Rosalie Maggio." Vernon left Taylor's office feeling better than he had in months. He was well-armed with a plan and clear direction. Taylor wasn't so bad after all, and now that she knew what he was up against, she was more likely to be lenient with him. He'd just need to refresh his old school ways.

Like Vernon, you may be experiencing the jet lag of technological acceleration. The stress and pressure you are feeling probably comes less from corporate policy and new technology than from your increasing awareness of the gap between your present skill level and the new requirements. Ignoring the cause of the stress will only increase the anxiety.

The gap in learning or training must be reduced or compensated for. But this cannot be done while blaming others, procrastinating, or denying the problem. Technology creates stress in other ways. Machines have taken on supervisory functions and perform more efficiently and heartlessly. Is the machine a better boss? Or does it, like its human counterpart, frustrate and enrage you? Television surveillance monitors scan our every activity from the front entrance to the cafeteria. In a few buildings even the restroom entrances don't escape the small round eye. What's next, company-mandated smartphones that actually track your every move?

The C-suite explains that the surveillance is for our own good, making us more efficient and safe. But is that true? Or do we run up costs using valuable time attempting to find ways to circumvent the system? Often we feel spied on and mistrusted. Most of us at some point take the intense scrutiny personally and resent the bosses who care nothing about invading our privacy. We feel monitored every moment, from entering the workplace until quitting time.

SPY EYES

The little red dot blinked as the TV camera scanned each work cubical. It didn't miss a square inch of the sales division. Junior and senior brokers had been outraged at this personal invasion of privacy since they first got word the cameras were to be installed. Everyone voiced their disapproval to management. It fell on deaf ears. Mcmos were sent with no reply. Most brokers agreed it might not be so intolerable if the surveillance was only visual. However, this eye in the sky was equipped with audio in each cubicle. Every word they said was transmitted to the legal department on the floor above.

An hour-long meeting had been held to explain the need for such a device to the brokers. The company attorney had said, "This surveillance is for your protection as well as our own. After all, you are trading in high-risk commodities options over the phone. We have the responsibility to ensure compliance with full disclosure is made to our investors." He ended his little speech by telling the brokers not to take it personally. "We are not here to spy on you."

"'We're not here to spy on you?' The hell they're not!" Marcus couldn't seem to get the statement out of his mind. At twenty-nine years old, he was a veteran trader. He had worked two years on the floor of the Chicago exchange prior to his move to California. He took the position at International Commodity Brokers because it was one of the most prestigious companies on the coast and his commission would put him in the six-figures-a-year bracket. Marcus was smooth, fast, and loved to talk. It was a job made in heaven. One of the perks he gave himself was free personal phone calls to his friends and family across the country, some overseas. In the past Marcus didn't care if his managers monitored his calls from time to time. The faint "click" on his line would warn him. He would quickly hang up.

Marcus had a problem. His computer was programmed with Tele-Magic. This meant he pressed the D key when a client file was brought up on the screen, and the number would be automatically dialed. The system not only saved the company time and money, it also kept an accurate record of the length and time of the call. Now if he called his friends, he had to dial manually. It had been easy to make his call before the spy-eye had been installed. All he did was wait until his manager either went to lunch or was occupied with other duties. Now he would have to find a way to beat the system. Not only was Marcus angry at the company for robbing him of his personal perk; he was even mad at the inventor of Tele-Magic.

He began to complain to his fellow brokers about their plight during the day, disrupting their concentration. After work, when he stopped to meet friends at the local pub, he spoke of nothing else. His friends were fast becoming bored with his whining. It would not take long before his career was affected too. Had Marcus stepped out of his anger for a few minutes and taken a reality check he might have found a humorous side to his situation. Here he was, a successful, young broker earning six figures a year. He owned lots of "toys," lived in a great apartment, and had six Armani suits hanging in his closet. He also had a company credit card and an iPhone purchased by the company. The rage he was experiencing was not because he couldn't make free phone calls at his desk anymore. It was because he felt the organization had taken away something that was his.

Vernon and Marcus had more in common with each other than you may think. Both were in the process of becoming casualties of the high-tech business world. What set them apart was the action they took. Each produced different results. Vernon used a constructive, open manner, confronting his own deficiency by revealing the problem openly to his boss. Together they devised a strategy for correction. Vernon would likely keep his job and progress.

Marcus was also confronted with his own deficiency. Instead of accepting responsibility for the situation that he created, he began to blame, criticize, and berate the company. As his coworkers became more and more irritated with his negativity, word got back to the boss. Eventually Marcus was fired. Marcus acted out in a destructive pattern that cost him his job.

As the life span of new technology shrinks, the rate of change accelerates exponentially. Bill is an example of an employee who resisted change. He ended up stranded on the information highway. Bill works for a large federal agency. Every month, the employees used to fill out paper travel vouchers, reporting their reimbursable expenses. Although somewhat tedious, most employees didn't mind the trouble it took to get their travel checks.

Then management introduced an automated travel-voucher system. Each employee was assigned a password to log into a centralized computer system where he or she entered itemized expenses. Travel checks were issued in a few days, instead of weeks. For most workers, the learning curve was short, and they were more than anxious to learn the new system because their checks arrived so much sooner.

For Bill, however, this new system became a major obstacle. He had never used a personal computer before and was comfortable with the old way, even though he wanted his check faster, too. But paper vouchers were no longer acceptable. His manager was tolerant at first, letting Bill impose on the secretary to enter his data into the system. Within three months, though, Bill was the only employee in the group who was not inputting his own travel information. The secretary began to complain about the additional burden. Finally, the manager laid down the law and told Bill he had to learn the new system. Begrudgingly, Bill entered his first month's travel with the help of the secretary. Although this first voucher took considerably longer to prepare than the old paper document would have, Bill felt both relieved and elated at having finally participated in the computer age.

In today's workplace, employees often experience stress as the need for technical skill increases. Whether the challenging situation is a software learning gap, a machine supervisor, or a surveillance camera in the lunch room, the question is the same: How do I take control?

STOP BEING A VICTIM

Begin by refusing to be a victim. In order to get out of the victim role, we must first identify the behaviors of powerlessness, sympathy-seeking, and irrational blame.

What's Your Victim Quotient?

Here is a short quiz to increase awareness and help you to look candidly at yourself. Answer the following yes or no questions:

1. Are you frequently worried about what might happen to you and your job?
2. Do you worry a lot about the future in general?
3. Do you often feel sorry for yourself because of your job situation?
4. Do you try to manipulate and control others around you by seeking sympathy, crying, or repeating stories of perceived abuse?
5. Do you dramatize events at work and blow them out of proportion?
6. Do you need lots of approval at work and gratitude for doing your job?
7. Do you resent your boss or the people you work with?
8. Do you find yourself whining and complaining about all the things that are wrong at work?
9. Do you blame your boss or other people at work for your unhappiness with your job?
10. Do you frequently remind yourself and others how much you are sacrificing and how hard you work for the company?

If you answered yes to:

Zero to two questions:	You're in pretty good shape; you are human.
Three to five questions:	You are bordering on victimhood.
Five to ten questions:	You see yourself as a victim. But it's not a terminal condition!

Stop Being a Victim

To end the powerlessness and blaming characteristics associated with the victim syndrome, first you need to understand that you have certain rights on the job. You need to know what they are and assume responsibility for them by standing up for yourself in a mature way. I mean more than just those covered by the labor laws. These are rights you have as an individual. You have the right to work in an environment that gives you a sense of your own personal power. Some of us have worked under poor managers for so long that we don't even know we have rights. Out of fear we let others walk over us; we permit others to mistreat us, and then we get back at them in subtle ways that are every bit as destructive as the mistreatment we experience.

The problem is that our rights are all too often not even acknowledged, much less honored. Some managers who are of the "us/them" mentality believe that, if people are too happy, they will take advantage of management and will not do the job. Discomfort, they contend, is a sure cure for happiness.

Start with slowing things down. Consider these statements:

1. This change isn't comfortable, but I can accept it.
2. I can have negative feelings (sadness, pain, anxiety) and still deal with the situation.

3. This is not an emergency. It's okay to slow down. I can take time to think things through. I will acknowledge my feelings and then move on.
4. Just because I don't like something doesn't mean it is bad or that it will hurt me. (Change may just be like lima beans.)
5. It's okay to have angry thoughts. I do not have to act on them.
6. I have the right to make mistakes. I don't have to do it right the first time. Nobody else is perfect, either.
7. I have the right to say how I feel.
8. I can say I don't know, and I have the right to ask for help.
9. Practice the statement, "You could be right;" "You are right;" you may even progress to the dreaded, "I was wrong."

As you reduce your victim quotient and increase your self-esteem, you will, by definition, become more assertive. Assertive behavior is not anger or acting out. It combines the expression of feeling and honesty with sensitivity and concern for the other person's feelings. The goal of assertiveness is not to change you. Rather, the purpose is to give you yet another tool that you can use and put away when you have finished with it. Assertive behavior is used to resolve conflicts, to bring about a change in another person's behavior, or to alter a situation.

JUST FOLLOWING ORDERS

It is normal and wise to anticipate certain negative responses to assertive behavior. The other person might become angry, or get their feelings hurt, or be afraid you don't like them: "What if they try to get even? What if I get fired?" You may fear retribution. Common sense has not been abandoned because you picked up another tool from your toolbox. Temper your use of new behaviors until you have gained some mastery. You can tolerate anger, hurt feelings, and other responses. Those create further opportunities for communication and ultimately may increase the rapport and intimacy with the other person. If you are truly afraid of retribution, then some outside consultant such as a minister or friend may be in order. But the goal is to adapt, which reduces legitimate discomfort and can help to allay fears. Accepting change while being assertive can give you both respect and support under difficult circumstances. Remember, you have a right to your feelings, and you have a right to ask for changes in another person's behavior. And just as technology acts without borders, your rights are always in effect.

Keisha sat at her desk in the accounting department. It was 6 A.M. and still dark when she arrived at work. Now at 8:30 A.M. she was still putting the finishing touches on the monthly statements. Mr. Fletcher wanted them for the morning staff meeting. "Damn!" she said, "I wish he would be more consistent with his directions. Yesterday morning he said he didn't need the report, then just before quitting time, he emailed me saying he wanted the spread sheets no later than 10 A.M."

The hard part of her task was getting used to the new accounting system programmed only last week. Although Keisha was computer literate, with a solid accounting background, the abrupt changes in systems confused her. What bothered Keisha most were the changes that came without notice or a plan for implementation. Just when she had mastered one program, Mr. Fletcher would introduce something new, with the promise that it would make her job easier and more effective.

Keisha was aware that she had talent and was a competent accountant. However, lately she had started to question her abilities to keep up with the pace. She reflected back to the time she had joined RAMCO Media Productions two years ago. She had been impressed with the company because of its clear vision and purpose for future growth.

Mr. Fletcher, her boss, was a brilliant man in his early forties. He was a true entrepreneur, fond of saying how he put up the money and took the risks. Mr. Fletcher took after technology, moving fast, talking fast, and making decisions even faster. Employees were given exceptional training, tools, and equipment to maximize their efficiency.

Keisha had liked working with energetic people in her office. Working for a high-tech, cutting-edge organization was exciting too. Now, behind schedule most of the time, she couldn't seem to stay on top of her workload. She felt as if she was on the freeway driving 80 miles per hour, and the cars were still passing her. The job was affecting other parts of her life. What used to be relaxing weekends had become a brief rest stop between Friday and Monday. All day Saturday her mind was occupied with tasks still on her desk at the office. By mid-afternoon on Sunday her anxiety erupted, a feeling she described as a heavy flutter in her chest and shortness of breath. Her mind raced and pains set in. "How will I get through tomorrow? What new program will I have to learn? What about the work I have completed? Will I have to toss it out?" Keisha has begun to dread Sunday nights. Meditation, counting backward from one hundred, or deep breathing would not quiet her mind and allow her to sleep. The alarm clock became her enemy. *Do any of my coworkers feel like this?*

Keisha's thoughts returned to the present. The spreadsheets were ready. What a relief. Looking up she saw Mr. Fletcher standing at the entrance to her cubicle. "Good morning, Mr. Fletcher," Keisha said. "I was just about to bring you the spreadsheets."

"Spreadsheets?" he replied. "That won't be necessary. We're not going to use them. I have another idea for the meeting this morning."

Frustrating? Infuriating? You bet! Can Keisha survive in the atmosphere of a fast-track, high-tech company? Maybe, maybe not. Still, she had some choices available. She could have resigned and found a less stressful employer. She could have arranged an appointment for a conference with Mr. Fletcher and explained how his management style affected her. He might have changed. Most likely he wouldn't. One option would be for Keisha to surrender, to cease resisting, stop the struggle, and give up the battle. Keisha didn't like to be pulled off track. It was upsetting for her to work inconsistently. She took pride in completing her tasks and owning the project, a fine trait in a worker but not appreciated at RAMCO. Mr. Fletcher was a mover and shaker; he would frequently say, "I put up the money and take the risks." It would serve Keisha well to give up her attachment to her projects and cease resisting the changes, accepting Mr. Fletcher's directions. It was not her company; she was paid to follow orders well, not to second-guess the commander.

CEASE FIRE

Surrender and release are powerful tools. Throughout history sages have told us of their value as the keys to peace and harmony. Their positive results have been proven time and time again. Knowing when and how to use these tools is important. We should incorporate them into our daily lives as often as needed to regain our balance.

When you feel pressure building inside you, stop for a moment. Ask yourself these important questions: What exactly am I holding on to? A project? An idea? An expectation? After identifying the sources for your upset, question yourself again: Why is this important to me? Why do I feel I must hold on? What value do I receive from holding on? Do I want to be right or get the job done? Have I fallen into a victim mode? When you have answered the last question you will be in a position to release. Using assertive behavior may help you move on. Let go. The process is simple, but not easy. With practice and patience it won't be difficult.

Armed with these tools, Keisha can work more comfortably with a boss like Mr. Fletcher in a fast-changing organization. She can view the challenge of new programs as a learning experience instead of as barriers to her production. She can think in terms of forward progress and exciting new ways to grow. Keisha will be like the artist, working with enthusiasm and freshness, eager for the next new battle.

Like Keisha, those of us who are facing the 21st century workplace have heard the saying, "The only thing that's constant is change." Industry must change and grow to maintain its competitive edge in today's global marketplace. Similarly, we too must adapt if we are to flourish. We cannot be resistant to change if we are going to survive. By availing ourselves of the new technologies as they appear on the horizon, we will not only progress individually, but we will make our work easier in the process.

Take It Back

Recognize

1. List the challenges you have now.
2. Write down some of the things that would be helpful to you in learning.
3. Figure out what you need to do to bring yourself up to speed (attend seminars, read books, take an online course).
4. What feelings do you attach to these challenges?

Respond

1. Buy a journal to record your feelings and reactions in regard to lack of control, powerlessness, and dysfunctional roles.
2. Decide to upgrade your job skills through a class, career counseling, or tutoring.

3. Consider getting more information on stress management—a book, a class, the EAP, or other avenues for personal growth.

4. Dialogue with yourself:

- Am I doing my best work?
- Do I expect my boss or coworkers to change?
- Do I expect the company to change?
- Do I want more encouragement?
- Do I want more training?

5. Listen more carefully to others. Notice that you may be responding when you don't need to. Wait for questions to be asked.

Reinforce

1. Try making these statements to yourself:

- I ask questions and express my feelings directly.
- Today I listen. I have the strength to be still.
- I can learn new skills. I can be exactly what I want to be.
- I am valuable. I am more valuable as part of a team.

2. Make ten easily-accessible notes on your smartphone with phrases your boss uses that make it hard for you to cope with the job. Then below it, write down your prepared answers. You will then be able to respond when the occasion arises. For example, "When you raise your voice, I feel like a little kid," or "There's something I want to say, and I need your agreement that you will listen, not react."

ELEVEN

BULL'S-EYE

"If you don't know where you are going, you will surely arrive there."
Ann D. Clark, Ph.D.

As creative human beings, we have the need to search and reach for new challenges in our lives. We are constantly planning a vacation, a family, a different home. As curious creatures we want to know and learn. We are challenged to learn to speak a new language or drive a car, to relax more or develop more patience. As visionaries we dream of a future free from family worries, financial problems, and self-doubt. In moments of insight, we make promises to ourselves to be more, do more, and have more. But very often these are promises we don't carry out.

Remember all those New Year's resolutions you forgot by Valentine's Day? Or those times when you swore, "I have to change my ways"? How about that new skill you were going to perfect, or that diet you've been on since those awkward teenage years? What happened to the idea about opening your own business, or becoming an author? For whatever reason we made these promises to ourselves—out of desperation or with good intention—we often give them up as quickly as we make them. Why do we give up our dreams so easily?

TO ERR IS GREAT

We view mistakes as a sign of failure, forgetting that errors are essential to our learning process. If we possessed all knowledge, there would be no need for schools or teachers. If

170

we were equipped with all skills, practice would be unnecessary. When research scientists make errors, they are called experiments. From each error valuable lessons are learned that further advance the research. The process is examined, and the errors are used to determine the design of the next procedure. Each experiment leads closer to the intended results. Success is not defined by the elimination of all the errors, but rather as progress toward a goal.

Sports provide a similar model. Athletes use losses, training lapses, criticism as motivation to train harder, to try again, and to improve technique. They hold on to the goals and dreams. Yet most of us are more often defeated by slips and self-defined failures. Too often we fail to allow ourselves room for mistakes. We abort our project and abandon the goal at the first missed shot.

Millions of people begin new diets each day only to give them up by noon. Ms. Dieter happens to slip up and munch a piece of candy at 10:15 A.M. Instead of getting right back on track, she may abandon the whole diet saying, "It's no use, I blew it." If you don't spend every waking moment zealously aiming toward your target, so what? Take the loss in stride and stay the course. When a jet is guided by radar, it flies only a theoretical straight line. In fact, it veers, errs perhaps, constantly correcting to remain on course. Jets may be seen as off course 90 percent of the time, yet they are always moving in the right direction. Sailboats, too, waver back and forth in the channel to find the wind. If you begin to drift off course, you may have to make adjustments to get where you're going. Continue to correct your course and keep your attention on the goal you have set.

Having done an evaluation of yourself as an employee, your company, your boss, and your coworkers, now is the time to implement changes into your job, your attitude, and your behavior. From a list of the Take It Back action steps and changes you can design an action plan. Try to accomplish some small steps each day. Evaluate the ones that don't work, and renegotiate with yourself. Put off some steps for later action.

Prioritize your goals according to importance and immediacy. Select the action steps needed to achieve the goals. Take the smallest steps first to gather momentum. Be ready to receive others' responses. Be open to praise and compliments as well as negative responses. Remember that as you change, others will struggle to keep you from doing so. Reevaluate your goals regularly. Share your achievements, however small, with trusted supporters.

ISOLATION TRAPS

Be persistent. Stick with the process. People may not want to change or see you change. They may be invested in the way you are. Your poor performance may make them look good. Codependency may be useful to them. When you begin working better, faster, smarter, others may feel threatened. Avoid the critics and wet blankets. Find cheerleaders instead. Letting coworkers know you are working on a self-improvement plan may reduce perceptions of threat. Enlist support. Ask for suggestions and learn from them, both what to do and what not to do. Motivation is the key to perseverance. Your success begins when you start; there is no end. Success is a rolling stone that can keep on going as long as momentum is provided.

"Sure," you say, "I'm all fired up now, but what about six months from now? How can I keep going?" Motivation is the byproduct of desire. Think about the ends, not the means. Few want cottage cheese and carrot sticks for lunch: it is the vision of washboard abs or pictures of a trimmer you that provides motivation. Again, use planning and process to create motivation at those times when work mounts up, tempers flare, or organizational charts start circulating. Avoid the isolating and demotivating traps of bad habits, comfort zones, denial, groupthink, or the general press of life. See your goals as the bull's-eye on a dartboard. Identify your target and hit it.

Melissa had been with the same company for over five years and had held four different positions. When she moved to marketing, the grapevine opinion was that she had finally met a manager who wouldn't put up with her attitude and poor performance. True enough. After 30 days she was written up, after 45 she was in human resources and referred to the EAP, and after 60 days she was put on last-chance probation. Five days into the probation she was fired.

One problem with Melissa was her feeling of entitlement. She felt, after five years of service to the company, that no one would fire her. Her example proved to her coworkers that length of service does not equal job security. During her exit interview, Melissa complained that none of her previous bosses had ever confronted her performance. In actuality, none of them had done so on the record or directly to her. And supervisors are human, too. Taking risk, being too lenient, codependency, and more can be issues.

But ultimately, Melissa knew she had a problem. The problem was her own denial, lazy habits, and rationalization that made her continue to underperform and ultimately become a surprised victim. One option suggested by the EAP was to have several coworkers doing jobs similar to Melissa's coach her for several hours during the day. She needed to revamp her attitude, her behavior, and her skills. Melissa preferred to stick with her victim posture.

Jane worked for an alcoholic boss. He would be normal for several months and then begin drinking at lunch or in the morning. Jane began to notice and finally spoke of the behavior to coworkers who said it had been going on for years. He was a partner in the company, so nothing could be done. Jane began to resent her boss, to disrespect him, and finally to despise him. She texted during work, slammed doors, lost messages, was rude, and considered calling the police to catch him drinking and driving on his way home.

Eventually, one of the other partners took Jane aside and let her know that if her disrespectful behavior continued she would be terminated. Jane had to do something to come to terms with her emotional turmoil. She had to learn to accept her boss, to respect him again, the way she had when she first started the job. The first step for Jane was to admit that her behavior had to change. Her job was at stake, not his. She could not change her boss, but she could change her attitude, her perceptions, and her actions.

Jane learned to act professionally. Her focus on professionalism allowed her to see how her own behavior could change. She asked herself how she would act if the problem was not alcohol but simply a difficult personality. She began to look at her position as a career and a challenge rather than just a job in which she was powerless. This, rather than her boss's appreciation, became her motivation for quality and excellence.

Jane began to attend Al-Anon meetings and learned how to accept her alcoholic boss and get on with her job. She learned to set boundaries and limits. She listened to stories from others who had overcome similar problems. Looking back, Jane feels grateful to her former boss. "If it had not been for his drinking problem, I would not have had the impetus to work on my own issues. The experience was a challenge that taught me a lot about survival."

Create affirmations like Jane did and repeat them daily with real feeling (or fake it 'til you make it): "Today I will find joy in my work!"

RECOGNIZING ALLIES

But sometimes there are jobs or situations that cannot be remedied. Efforts to change become a greater struggle. Things continue to happen that seem to be out of your control. Pressure mounts, last-minute crises arise, appointments are missed, papers get misplaced, and projects are covertly sabotaged.

Hedy was the office manager of a small, thriving business. She talked many times about getting married and moving out of the state. Run-ins with her boss were becoming more frequent, and she was having trouble getting along with the rest of the staff. One of Hedy's duties was to coordinate the inter-office communication system. On hearing about the proposed new phone equipment, she protested vehemently, saying that such a change wasn't necessary, that it would be too complicated for the staff, and that the old system was quite adequate.

But the company installed the system, and a phone company representative came to instruct the staff on its usage. Hedy was noticeably absent for most of the session, home with a cold. When she did attend, she seemed disinterested, hostile, and would not interact with the trainer. Once left on her own, Hedy could not handle the new phone system. Long-distance callers were cut off and had to be contacted again. Phone lines were out of service for hours at a time. Calls were crossed. Confusion reigned. Stress levels rose. Callers became irate, resulting in business losses.

Hedy was ultimately fired. At some level she knew her unwillingness to open her mind created chaos. Her desire to be somewhere else left her mind scattered. Had she accepted the new vision instead of drawing a line in the corporate sand, the changeover could have been much smoother, and Hedy could have been a hero. Everyone concerned could have been saved the grief, stress, and confusion. But she could not retarget, and it resulted poorly for Hedy.

MOVING ON

Are you fed up? Angry? Disillusioned? Perhaps your needs have not been met or you can't see any future to your job. Okay, quit. You have that right. Before you slam the door behind you, overloaded with a cardboard box of photos and old calendars, give this decision-making exercise a try.

First take a legal-size piece of paper and draw a line down the middle, from top to bottom. On the right side of the paper write down everything you like about your job. Now on the left write down everything you perceive as being wrong—those things that do not meet your needs. When you have finished you will have enough information to make a conscientious choice.

If your decision is to leave, make sure you cover yourself by doing the best work in the time you have left. It can pay off with a good recommendation. Do your job search on personal computers, not the company's. If you don't, you may find yourself leaving sooner than planned. Your coworkers may overhear and inform your supervisor just to score points, and these days computers are always monitored. Besides, it's dishonest. You're still on the payroll. When you were hired you sold your time—the company bought it. Make phone calls on your lunch hour or break, and do so outside the building. Send emails and resumes to potential employers after work. Plan ahead when you're ready to resign. Inappropriate actions now will only hurt you down the road. Be professional by writing your letter of resignation. Give careful consideration to your personal career needs before stating your decision. Give at least two weeks' notice. Don't be surprised if you are asked to leave immediately and told you can pick up your personal items. There may even be a stern security guard. Be prepared financially. Don't count on the extra two weeks' pay. Know your state regulations and company policy.

Don't feel guilty about leaving or letting the company down. Take care of yourself first. Someone will fill the position. Hopefully you made a positive difference while employed. Carry all your good qualities to the next position. The company is impersonal; coworkers are not. Don't leave them with a mess to clean up. Quit with dignity and honor for yourself and the possibility of future jobs. Start the next position clean, fresh, and feeling good. But no matter how long you choose to stay with a job, it's important to be objective. In business, as in life, it's easy to become complacent, to go with the flow. But isn't it better to be in control?

So look at the big picture. Set recurring reminders in your phone to do a job evaluation in the months of January and June. There's nothing wrong, and everything right, with reviewing the job, your boss, the people you work with, and maybe even yourself. You may be surprised about what you learn. There are no rules, so be creative. You're in control of your own feelings. Ask some tough questions, and answer truthfully: How do I feel about my job? What am I doing? Is everything okay here? Am I being treated well? Am I financially sound? Can I do better? Do I want more? Is this a healthy environment?

A problem is usually a gift in disguise, if you are willing to recognize it as such. If you've been hanging on to a job you no longer want, you're probably creating many of the challenges you've been having with your boss or your coworkers. If you're tired of the relationship, you may find more and more irritations creeping in. Discomfort in life can bring awareness into conscious thought.

Like a tragic love story, when you know, you just know when to quit. You might fantasize about quitting your job daily because you just can't make things work with your boss, your job, the people, or you feel you're wasting your time. Jennifer, a junior account executive at a top public relations firm, was always working hard and took pride in perfecting every job at an efficient pace. But her boss, Mr. Epstin, always second-guessed her work at every turn. He would give preference to the male junior account executives. It didn't help that Jennifer was currently the only female. Jennifer tells us about her breaking point: "I was preparing for a presentation with one of our huge Fortune 500 clients and our executives. I was ecstatic with the opportunity; I figured this was finally my big break. Mr. Epstin was actually giving me a chance. I worked around the clock for two months on this presentation, memorized it backwards and forwards so I could present it in my sleep if I had to.

"The day before the presentation, Mr. Epstin approached me and abruptly said, 'Please explain all your notes to Garrett.

He will be giving the presentation tomorrow, so don't forget to set it up for him in the morning.'

"Several colorful curses flooded my mind, but I was at a loss for words! All that work, just to let Garret take all the credit. Suddenly my quitting fantasies came roaring back. I thought, 'Maybe I can key his Jaguar with I QUIT! Or I can get a church choir to come in and sing Glory Hallelujah, I QUIT!'

"I couldn't believe what was happening, but I was pretty sure it had to do with the fact that I had mountains on my chest and a valley between my legs. I graduated top from my class at UPenn, and I was a huge asset to the company, but since I started this job all I could think about was how to take it out on my boss when I quit. Maybe I had expected to fail. I knew the only other female junior account executive transferred locations because she knew she would not excel here. But I was not going out without a bang—and making sure everyone knew what kind of chauvinistic pig my boss is.

"So I did what was I was told. I taught Garrett everything I knew about the presentation. The next day I set up the newly prepared PowerPoint presentation in the conference room for all the executives, including the CEO, and our client. Then simply left, I mean literally left the office. I relished in imagining the looks on Garret's and Mr. Epstin's faces toward the end of the PowerPoint presentation, when I had carefully inserted a picture of Mr. Epstin as a winning example of the company's Etiquette and Ethics Guidelines highlighting Gender Inequality."

I recently saw a meme online that read, "The next best thing to quitting my job is fantasizing about quitting my job." There's an important moral here: when it's time to move, start packing. Don't let resentments build unaddressed. After Jennifer left, she was unlikely to get a winning recommendation letter from her boss who she had worked for for three years. That's three years down the drain—three years she was nervous to list as a reference for her work experience, despite her dedicated work ethic. Most of the time, minor workplace conflicts can be solved, but when they can't, it doesn't behoove you to take the company in flames down with you. That old saying about not burning those bridges? It's always right.

"Clarity comes from *action*, not thought." I love this quote from Marie Forleo on Derek Halpern's Social Triggers site. In a talk about how to stop self-sabotage, they stress that excuses will only lead you into a spiral of defeat. In the preceding chapters the labyrinth of wartime politics have been explored: bosses, management, anger, resentment, self-management, and of course hopes and dreams. If it is time to go, then go. Often making the decision to leave, voicing it to family and friends, creates a sense of relief and renews the energy needed to target a new job—a new vision for you. In making the decision to move on, it is necessary to be rigorously honest. Tell the truth about what you are and are not willing to do. If the task, whatever it may be, honestly, seems hopeless, let it go. If, like Hedy, you are not willing to change in the workplace, move on rather than resist. Give yourself permission to stay as you are and take a next step. If you are not willing to take the risks you perceive as necessary to gain control, let that be a statement of self-understanding, not self-criticism. Finding your niche then becomes the target.

TARGET PRACTICE

But whether the job is overwhelming, or you are really determined to make your work *work*, you do need a goal. Often, the target may change along the way. You may start out wanting to quit. But then as you become more aware of the workplace war going on around you, you may begin to work toward peace and learn to find joy in your job again.

Think of targeting as a circular process. You begin by choosing a specific goal or target; develop the action steps, and visualize targeting as a flexible process. Here's an example. Mary says, "I want to get my real estate license. My plan is to go to real estate school and pass the state exam." Next she takes action by carrying out the first step of her plan. She enrolls in school and completes her first three classes. By the third class Mary feels the material is too difficult for her to learn. She misses the next class because of her son's birthday party, and by the fifth class, she thinks she's too far behind to catch up.

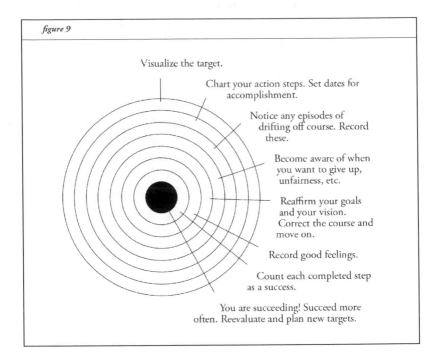

figure 9

Visualize the target.

Chart your action steps. Set dates for accomplishment.

Notice any episodes of drifting off course. Record these.

Become aware of when you want to give up, unfairness, etc.

Reaffirm your goals and your vision. Correct the course and move on.

Record good feelings.

Count each completed step as a success.

You are succeeding! Succeed more often. Reevaluate and plan new targets.

Mary feels like quitting but decides not to give up. She reaffirms her goal and continues with her studies. She doesn't label her difficulty as failure. She visualizes herself closing big deals. She feels better about herself for going through the barrier, and to her surprise, the real estate course begins to make more sense. She completes her studies and passes the exam. Mary confidently plans her new target: "Now I want to work for the most productive real estate company in town."

Perseverance is an admirable quality. However, there is a difference between persevering and being stubborn. If your dream begins to turn into a nightmare, stop. Take a long, hard look at what you're doing. If you have been unrealistic, reevaluate. Is your plan adversely affecting your physical well-being or mental health? Are you experiencing more instead of fewer problems? Do minor irritations upset you more than they used to? Do you cry more often? Is your goal affecting your home life? Are you having frequent arguments with your family? It's time for you to reassess your situation. You may have to give up that goal for now. More likely, you will be able to overcome the problems by altering your method or practicing more flexibility in your plans.

Consider a football game. A specific target is designated. All the players are in agreement as to the goal. The quarterback calls the play. A long, downfield pass may get there quickly, but there are obstacles along the way. On the football field, they are called defensive backs, free safeties, and defensive linemen. When running into (or passing into) these obstacles, the quarterback may elect to throw a short, sideline pass. It may look as if the team is off course. If the game plan works, eventually the target is reached. Just as in football, when you are targeting, you may have to alter strategies, go for the short pass or kick a field goal, or even give the other team a go briefly.

Acquiring the Target

Many times we don't take the time to design a plan of action. We haven't worked out the day-by-day steps to achieve the intended result. Lacking a plan, we may also lack sufficient commitment. Without a plan, commitment, and the steps to move toward a goal, we may not understand what's required to attain our results. We give in to frustration and confusion. As we search for an easier, softer way, we become fatigued. We would rather quit than risk what we have visualized as failure. It seems easier to give up. Often we overlook the most important factor in reaching our targets—a clear picture of what we want to accomplish. Remind yourself of the rewards. Literally draw a picture of yourself where you want to be. Put that picture where you see it daily. The bathroom mirror is a good choice. Remind yourself that motivation is the byproduct of desire. As you increase the desire for your goal, motivation is also increased.

You're More than a Pawn

The benefits you will gain from working your Basic Plan, the beginning of the targeting process, are numerous. First, the benefits are not primarily seen in changes on the job but in how you feel about yourself. The gains in self-esteem are the most valuable of all. You will find release from anger, from resentments turned inward, and from depression turned outward. You will gain a renewed sense of self-honesty and your own values, standards, and personal morality. You will no longer be working against your own value system. You'll feel repaired.

As you progress in targeting and accomplishing your action steps, you will feel in greater control of your emotions and less affected by the actions, attitudes, and opinions of others. Instead of leading with your emotional chin, you are now executing a series of planned, controlled moves. In the language of boxing, you're displaying some fancy footwork and you're less likely to be hit.

Through empowerment you will gain increased control—if only in your perception. It is likely you will have gained increased control over your work environment. You will influence and persuade others more effectively and find yourself more productive, not only on the job, but in the personal and social spheres of your life as well. Recognize, Respond, and Reinforce by being honest with yourself, evaluating the situation, seeking answers, and having specific targets. Who knows? You might inspire your coworkers and even—really—your bosses to Take it Back and bring peace to the workplace.

BIBLIOGRAPHY

Adams, Douglas. *The Salmon of Doubt.* New York: Random House, 2005.

Alcoholics Anonymous. *The Big Book.* 3rd Ed. Alcoholics Anonymous World Services, 1976.

Bramson, R. *Coping with Difficult People.* Anchor Press, 1981.

Clark, Ann D. *Women & Recovery: Sex, Sobriety, & Stepping Up.* iUniverse, 2013.

Covey, Steven. *The Seven Habits of Highly Effective People.* Free Press, 2004.

Fensterheim, H. and J. Baer. *Don't Say Yes When You Want to Say No.* Dell Books, 1975.

Fisher, R. and W. Ury. *Getting to Yes: Negotiating Agreement Without Giving In.* Penguin Books, 1983.

Folger, J. and M. Poole. *Working Through Conflict: A Communication Perspective.* Scott Foresman, 1984.

Follman, J. F. *Helping the Troubled Employee.* Amacom, 1978.

Forbes, B.C. *Keys to Success.* 1917.

Forleo, Marie and Derek Halpern. *Beaten by Self Sabotage? Marie Forleo Shows You How To Fight Back.* YouTube Video. Social Triggers, 2012. http://socialtriggers.com/self-sabotage-marie-forleo/ (accessed May 17, 2013).

Gardner, John W. *Self-Renewal: The Individual and the Innovative Society*. New York: W. W. Norton & Company, 1995.

Harmon, Frederick G. *The Executive Odyssey: Secrets for a Career Without Limits*. John Wiley and Sons, 1989.

Harragan, Betty Lehan. *Games Mother Never Taught You: Corporate Gamesmanship for Women*. Warner Books, 1977.

Harrs, T. A. *I'm OK—You're OK*. Harper & Row Publishers, Inc., 1973.

Henry J. Kaiser Family Foundation. "Snapshots: Health Care Spending in the United States & Selected OECD Countries." 12 Apr. 2011. Kff.org.

Hootman, Marcia, and Patt Perkins. *How to Forgive Your Ex-Husband*. Doubleday, 1982.

Jobs, Steve. "Stay Hungry. Stay Foolish." Keynote speech, Stanford University Commencement, Stanford, June 12, 2005.

MacKay, Harvey. *Swim With the Sharks Without Being Eaten Alive*. William Morrow, 1988.

Marston, W. M. *Emotions of Normal People*. Persona Press, 1979.

Peck, M. S. *The Road Less Traveled: A New Psychology of Love, Traditional Values and Spiritual Growth*. Simon & Shuster, 1978.

Schaef, Anne Wilson. *The Addictive Organization: Why We Overwork, Cover Up, Pick Up the Pieces, Please the Boss, and Perpetuate Sick Organizations*. New York: HarperOne, 1990.

Sprouse, Martin and Tracy Cox. *Sabotage in the American Workplace: Anecdotes of Dissatisfaction, Mischief, and Revenge.* San Francisco: Pressure Drop Press, 1992.

Wells, T. *Keeping Your Cool Under Fire: Communicating Non-Defensively.* McGraw-Hill, 1980.

Woititz, Janet. *Adult Children of Alcoholics.* Health Communications, Inc., 1983.